THE ICE-FLOE GIRL

The Ice-Floe Girl

Published by The Conrad Press in the United Kingdom 2020

Tel: +44(0)1227 472 874
www.theconradpress.com
info@theconradpress.com

ISBN 978-1-913567-34-7

Typesetting:
Charlotte Mouncey, www.bookstyle.co.uk

The Conrad Press logo was designed by Maria Priestley.

Printed and bound in Great Britain by Clays Ltd, Elcograf S.p.A.

The Ice-Floe Girl

Gregory Motton

Lotta

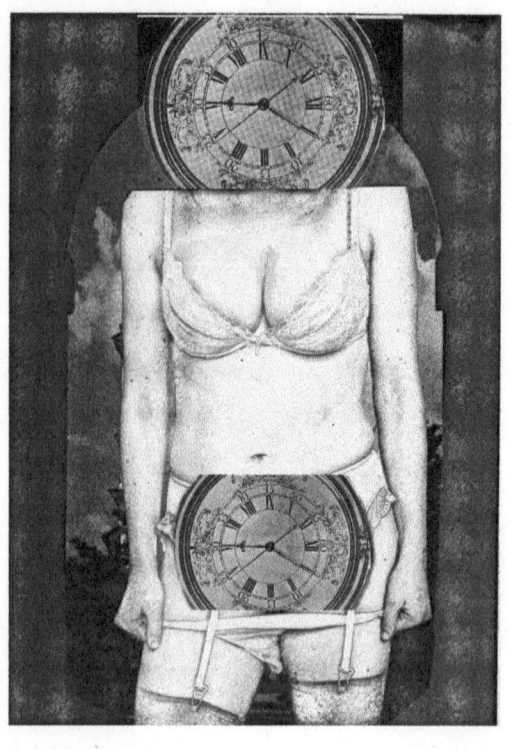

1

I was sitting in a pub near my parents' house with a childhood friend. He and I were about to leave the pub to go on one of our Friday evening walkabouts, moving garden gnomes, exploding litter bins and hanging communist flags from our suburban railway bridge, and other childish entertainments; a girl, Sarah, came into the pub whom we half knew, well enough for her to feel slightly awkward not saying hello, or even perhaps offering to join us. With her, an apparition, who turned out to be a Swedish au pair. Immediately I prayed they would join us, and they did. They had come out for a walk because, they said, they were bored with sitting at home in Sarah's parents' house. Our little suburb was quiet, rather idyllic, a classic suburb with lawn-mowers, half naked vicars, and a badminton club in the 1920s wooden church hall. We all loved it really, I was sad my parents were moving out and I was of course having to move out too, not with them because they were leaving London, but a little further down the train line, towards the centre of London, past the communist-flagged bridge into the real world.

The apparition sat to my left at a right-angle to me. I am left handed, it was a good omen, sinister and propitious.

Her face was a phenomenon. It cleared the decks. One look

at it and I was ship-shape and ready for a life-time's voyage of devotion. Such clarity and mildness I had never seen. Other girls had skin, this creature was wrapped in mist. Other beauties had features which were nevertheless human, all too human, maybe loveable for their sheer humanity. This girl's face was unblemished by any strength of feature, even though each one of them was of exceptional prettiness, for their pale easiness drew an ethereal veil over them which soothed the mind and would have brought peace to any troubled soul.

Her actual features, as far as any mind could perceive them individually, were:

Bright blue eyes of only moderate size, whose irises were so resolutely blue they could look brown, eyes that were without much shadow or depth, and which had perfectly, delicately formed eyebrows over them, and pale brown lashes. I won't try to describe her glance, for that would be to depart from a merely physical description and to sail towards the heart or mind or psyche, and I only suffered the wild glint of their axe three times that evening, and my blood was frothing with adrenalin as a consequence the whole time she was sitting there.

Her mouth was a blessing, the envy of all, the kind that has become the expensive, dangerous aim of ambitious beauties, for it was of the full-lipped kind. When it was closed, it was drawn sweetly into a finely-painted perfection that was demure and kind and of the first order of beauteousness; when it was open or in motion, it was slightly lascivious, indeed it had a tenancy to remain partly open in a kind of sudden vacancy which was increased by her slightly prominent, large and regularly shaped teeth over which her upper lip was also prominent when open or talking. It was a mouth men dream of, it was the mouth of obscenity, made for salacious fantasy, a mouth that could launch a thousand waves on a wine-dark sea, a mouth from which I looked away, not wanting to stare and give my thoughts away.

Her nose confounded likelihood for, notwithstanding her other good features, she had been also granted the prettiest of noses, a small, upward-sloping, ski-slope, gently pointed nose, that was rounded and pointed at the same time as if to give a choice or to create an impossible blend. The upward pointing nose is a common enough Swedish characteristic, but hers was without fault or concession, as if the rest of her face had demanded the best nose possible to go with it, and had been granted it.

Her face seen from the front was very young and round and faint in its gentle impression of sweetness, while in profile it was voluptuous and seductive and bewitching.

From the front her expression was naïve, open and alert and fresh, while in profile, her blue eyes turned dark, and the relationship between her full lips, moist and shining, and her upwards nose gave a shocking and surprising impression of vacancy , licentiousness and wantonness.

Dimples adorned those cheeks. a last flourish of nature upon the surface of its work of art, or the common consequence of prominent teeth. Not a trace of makeup had ever been near that face, it was like a summer breeze from an unseen, untouched heath.

Her hair actually had two natural colours, mid brown with golden streaks, which I subsequently found to be the product of nothing other than the feeble Scandinavian sunshine, another blessing of good fortune. These two colours gave a feeling of silken ropes adorning a marble face, and hung to her shoulders, curling and twisting like a natural version of the rounded chords of silver and bronze, the carvings on a Viking sword hilt. She had the most extraordinary fringe, cut very short, dead straight but irregular and crooked, of a kind I had never seen before or since. On another face it might have looked harsh, but on this the softest and prettiest of faces it merely gave a comical and slightly child-like effect.

Her brow was not high and was the straight and flat and calm sort, typical of her race, the consummate adornment of her delicate face. She wore small round, golden glasses. She had the sweetest, prettiest, most beautiful, kindest most arousing and sexually provocative face I had ever seen.

I was conquered before a few minutes had passed.

She was rather quiet, her English was good but not at all idiomatic or fluent, it was formally correct. She was awkward and almost completely without spontaneity, and perhaps because of this, along with her actual appearance, gave an otherworldly impression. I actually kept looking behind me and around the pub to see if anyone else had noticed her and if someone wasn't already homing in to snatch her away from me.

Not to have fallen instantly in love with her would have been not only foolish and perverse, it would have been a dangerous insult to Destiny, God and any other commanding authorities, known as they are to be easily aroused to ire. And so I duly fell in love with Lotta, at first sight. This was clearly a life changing moment, one that I had not been prepared for. It was a matter of destiny, and I was aware that, in my psychic planning, this was meant to happen several years up ahead, when, after a long search, the golden prize would be given to me, for in those days, and in my childhood I had felt myself to be lucky and favoured by the gods.

Lotta had come along the path of Fate early; I recognised her straight away, despite being confused and unnerved by her astonishing beauty and unsettling attractiveness. Somewhere in my memory was the knowledge that the woman I loved would be foreign with light brown straggly hair like this. I was even worried that my future wife should be out on her own like this, looking like this, where anyone might see her, and even get the wrong idea. I was so young that falling in love with her was a bit like falling in love with myself.

It ought to take a whole lifetime to fall in love with someone, or at least; to fall in love with someone whose star is attached to your own. I was no longer who I had been a few minutes before, I had awoken to my life, my feet were off the ground, my gladness was unbounded. I was relieved and excited, thrown down from where I sat, from out of my grey sleep, and propped up like a dummy and told to start breathing but not knowing how; I was still a child and yet I couldn't deny it, - that unwittingly, before me sat the girl I was to know the best of all people on the earth, whom I was to take with me to the stars when its all over, the girl who was the great gift life had given to me, the fated, fabled one true love, adored above life itself, whom I would die for, whose very presence would come to be the essence of life itself, the source and foundation of all my lusts and the gratification of the same, the fantasy and the mystery, the magic number, the symbol and the sign, the idol of an idol-atrous life, the love, the soft embrace and the kindness to quell the stone cold universe, the beloved mother of four children, the comfort and hope of my children and I, the hearth and heart of our home, the voice that sends us happy to sleep and brings us gently and lovingly to wakefulness again, the warmer smile than any of God's mornings, the presence of safety and hope, the surpasser of all my wildest fantasies, the whore, the painting, the consolation for all failure, the thrill, the missing liveliness of life, the consolation for failed religion, failed career, the test, the ordeal, the trial, the flame that nearly destroys, the secret hidden and then revealed, the hidden crime, the trail through the mind, the dark secrets, the violence in a cellar, the recovery, the wild sea and then the harbour, the journey into catastrophe, and the coming home, the shipwreck, the barrel, the raft, the open sea of thirst and despair, the discovery in moonlight sand, the wreck, the salvage, the everyday and the only true mystery left to me. She sat there so mild and decent, blue and light brown, not much more than a child herself, flashing her one, two, three blows of an axe within her crazy dark pale eyes, small and neat, contained easily in a glance, slight and harmless, unknowing but known to me, even then.

By the time we left the pub to go to our homes, my life was mapping itself out for me. I floated out through the door, and then ran back, realising I didn't even know her name, I had forgotten it. She told me, I felt as if I had proposed. I floated home and listened to my friend's comments upon the beatific vision. I happen to have them on a reel to reel tape, to this day;

'She wasn't wearing a bra.'

He also said she was a communist. In the pub, he had even attacked her barely held opinions, and I had flown to her rescue. It all went very well.

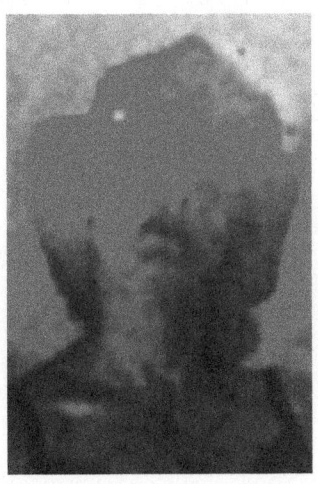

2

The days ran by, I thought I was going to see her. I never would have let her leave the pub if I hadn't been sure I would run into her. But I didn't. The end of December came and went, Christmas jingled past, she was nowhere to be seen.

By New Year's Eve I was getting desperate. I knew she was due to go back to Sweden on the fifth day of January. I persuaded my friend the communist flag hanging communist baiter, and his two brothers, to tour round the local pubs in search of her. We needed a car, we had to cover an area of a few miles square, even if she was in a local pub. As my friends pointed out, after the fifth pub, there was no reason to believe she would be.

'She's probably in Trafalgar Square with all the other au pairs.' Unable myself to drive, I was forced to keep a cool, persuasive head and tongue. Just one more, just one more. We drove around and around, my friends' patience and generosity wearing away as we drove. We stopped outside, I hopped out, ran in, took a look round, ran out again, at a series of pubs that were now filling up. We were in danger of not getting standing room. One last one! We whizzed to The Woodman, an old pub frequented by highwaymen in the 1700s, that was 300 yards from the house I was born in. This was now another turning point in my life; ....she wasn't there. Their patience had now ran out. A black curtain fell behind my eyes.

'Just one more? Please?'

To my relief, the car wheeled round and off we went, back to the first pub we had looked in, the same pub I had met her in two weeks ago. It took fifteen minutes to get there. I jumped out.

She was there in the car park, walking towards me, again with Sarah. A dog on a lead went for me. Lotta seemed very pleased to see me, she definitely recognised me anyway.

'We're taking Sarah's neighbours dog for a walk.' My mind wrestled with the information. I searched it for a plan. I found a party. Someone had mentioned one. I invited them, Sarah looked doubtful, Lotta said immediately yes. We walked in a procession to it. The dog was unloaded on the way. The party itself was a motionless icing-cake in my mind. Nothing moved, no sound was made. Lotta stood next to me. I knew I was on the way somewhere. Hours passed, bells rang, songs were sung, auld langsyne, we danced slow, my hand in her pocket. I was amazed how small she was compared to the space she took up in my mind. She told me she lived in a tree house, I kissed her on the cheek. She was gone.

I was left with a date. The next day but one. Life had begun.

Room 1, the National Gallery. A pink Giotto. I stared unseeingly at it, having seen it many times before. She came up behind me. This was it. She had turned up for our first date. Her golden halo merged with those on the walls, as she shimmered in the hushed reverence. She stared at the walls like someone who had never seen a painting before, amazed, almost without a clue. I stumbled around in front of her, leading her to new rooms. Her immense passivity was a like a lion raging about, I couldn't control it, or handle it, I was exhausted within five minutes. My mind was blank, my stomach was empty, hunger saved me from confusion. She spoke very little, I suggested we go and eat, and she was enthusiastic. Food, it seemed, was even better than paintings.

Unable to eat my lasagne, I watched her effortlessly eat a mountain of salad., I told her I was too nervous to eat, a confession, a declaration. The marriage altar grew nearer. We had exchanged maybe 1000 words by now, including at the party, 920 of them were mine.

Next stop the Essential Cinema Club, Soho. My regular haunt, foreign films, art films, *Fitzcaraldo* to *Intermezzo*, yes maybe even a Swedish film. I felt sure it would come up with something suitably exquisite for the occasion, although something was telling me this creature had never seen a film in her life. One thing was for certain, she was as foreign as a Chinaman.

The Harder They Come,' the ambiguity of the title didn't strike me until a few years ago. I don't think she noticed. She sat, her face, inscrutable, in the direction of the screen, but no image or word from the London Babylonian scene reached her, she was pristine. We decided to leave. She took me to a pub near where she had been an au pair, Dartmouth Park Hill, Highgate. This environment was familiar to her at least. She looked content in the quiet "grotty pub" as she had learnt to call it. She was as sweet as a puppy chasing a ball of wool. I wondered what time she had to be in.

As it turned out she was allowed out until whatever time she liked. We arrived to her friend Sarah's family at midnight. I didn't want them to stop her going out with me. A second kiss on the lips and she was gone. I walked home to Palmers Green, the place of pilgrims, along the railway tracks, clutching in my heart, the next date. Tomorrow. She had only two days left in London, she was on her way home.

She rang the door bell to the house I was living in, my bedsit was at the back, and I ran down the corridor, having waited with my ear to the wind, all afternoon, in case she would be left waiting on the door step. I could see her through the stained glass of the front door. She was down the step, a multicoloured small shape. I opened the door and nearly gasped at her love-liness. ushered her down the corridor, afraid it might seem unruly or ugly to her. She though, seemed to be a big fan of whatever I showed her, she grinned at me as if the house itself I had put there after trying to guess what she would like. Her approval was palpable but wordless.

She couldn't stay long, the family were all ready to take her touring London, as they had each day it seemed. It was embarrassing, she said, to suddenly be wanting to go out; they were all sitting waiting for her. I imagined them, holding an anorak for her, and a travel pass. I put the kettle on, she sat on my knee; my heart leapt, I could hardly believe it. I reached out and found a black Trilby hat, and put it on her head. She looked too good in it, I almost wanted to take it off to calm my nerves.

She looked around the mess from where she sat, and asked if I had been living here very very very long, a joke of such graceful deliberateness I wondered she hadn't given it to me wrapped in gold leaf. Apart from her sitting on my knee for a few minutes I was careful to keep away from her, as you would if the queen came to visit in your bedsit, not to alarm or impose. Within 30 minutes she was away to fulfil her duty as guest, and I was left nursing my happiness and the next appointment.

On our fifth and final meeting we had simply gone for a walk locally, around the suburb where I lived. We stood among the allotments and kissed demurely, romantically, as the pouring rain ran off our hair and down our foreheads and dripped off our noses. She seemed to like most when we didn't really do anything, and she was able to make a whole afternoon out of looking back out at me from the throne of her face, and issue proclamations of love with her eyes.

When we found ourselves accidentally on the deserted golf course, I suggested we sit down on the ground that was dry under a huge beach tree. She didn't want to, and I realised as we continued on our way, that she had wanted to avoid the possibility of hanky panky there on the ground. Personally I had not thought of it, but she had. I was charmed then by how prude she was. I felt as if only a girl from the nineteenth century would refuse to sit on the ground because of impropriety.

I took her home, we had been out all afternoon and evening doing and saying almost nothing, our time was almost up, there was a feeling of sadness and uncertainty. I could hardly bear to look at her. This time she asked me in. She had something in mind. After serving tea she took out an encyclopaedia and showed me a picture of Sweden; that was my cue;

'I'd love to go to Sweden.'

She invited me. The job was done, the evening could end. I almost wanted to rush away in-case it was undone somehow. She was on the sofa, more approachable than usual, by some strange mechanism of adjustment of the charisma.

She took off her glasses, for the first time. A curiously clumsy move. It was as if she thought I should see her properly before she left, maybe to make sure I actually went to Sweden. As if I needed further convincing on the appearance front. Nothing, not even my endless gawping at her could have prepared me. Her eyes were so weak and blue it was as if they would move away like clouds, and her nose was so delicate and pale, I had to squint to see if it was really there; I said something about her nose though, I said it had aqueducts, and it did. Aqueducts for tears, though I didn't say so. I kissed her lips, her flight home was approaching already, the night was gone, and morning was coming to take her away.

I had only seen Lotta five times. We were nineteen and I had arrived at the distant port and I had hardly left the harbour. That search which ought to take a part of a life, was fulfilled already. A sacred sort of creature, a mysterious spirit, a silent, untouched, new-born angel, from when Lucifer was still a favourite, she was deep and dark and crisp in the dark light, glowing like sleep, quiet like prayer, modest as a fairytale mouse, as green as grass and distant as the moon, as new as the earth is old, as light as blue eyes, as gay and as serious as wild flowers.

3

Her letters fell through the door, one, two, three; their large white squares, the stamps upside down, her handwriting curled and large like a nineteenth-century clerk's.

I sat in the chair, I stood in the hall, I lay in my bed, I waited in the kitchen; sausages, tea, ash and coal, she was there among them, her semi-holy presence, all gone away, to her foreign land where she had been invented, her language, her empty eyes, her pale, pale skin and dark shadow from within, lost on the sea, frozen in the snow, her boots of leather, her legs, her ski-slope nose –

The world was born again and she rose up from it, the new baby in woman form, a skinny girl, a giant goddess, a faint smile through prominent teeth, plain as a child, as beautiful as a painted courtesan, sunlight and dark, forbidding shadow met in her vanishing smile, and eyes that searched for escape but opened up to blue fields of gold and sun and rest and gentleness, her slow formal words on the page, friendly and plain, no mystery, no feminine wiles, the greatest female of them all, hidden from all, born upon the earth like a sprite made for love, her letter in my hand all day, just words, hardly read, too beautiful she is to see or know.

I had a little pink book, *Teach Yourself Swedish*; I studied the stamps, all line drawings of cars and animals and films, *Intermezzo,* graceful, unfamiliar words. I idled away the time in a trance waiting for six weeks to pass until I could visit her. I drank tea, one or two cans of beer, ate bacon and bread, smoked and read books, but mainly painted the walls, a trance-like life, inventing myself but now there was no need; the prize fell into my hands from the outset. I must be lucky.

I had only kissed her once, and she had sat on my knee. Such was her beauty I couldn't feel lust, even feeling the shape of her as she perched on my legs, I could only think 'Thank God for keeping me alive,' me a simple Catholic boy, good as gold, she a pagan goddess as bright as any sun. I thanked God for showing me the birth of nations, the beginning of history in her mythological face, belonging to the Viking race from another time. Yes she had sat on my knee but felt unlike any girl, her plain garments seemed like a miracle, their existence upon her person a blessing, like wings of iron, fresh, fresh air like the outside world as I had never known it, seemed to come like a breeze of breath from her skin.

Waiting for the weeks to pass I enjoyed my new life of living away from home, my parents having left town. I rented a back room in a large house in my suburb of London, an Edwardian house, with even a bit of stained glass in the back windows and large French doors opening to the neglected garden. With a friend from school, for I was recently a schoolboy, I painted the woodwork dark brown thinking to make it more Edwardian, and painted the walls grey.

Then it suddenly occurred to us to paint a red letter box, a whole pillar box, onto the wall, life size. It looked pretty good.

My friend was a painter, had just started at St Martin's School of Art on Charring Cross Road, and I could paint quite well too; we were so pleased that we added a palm tree and then a desert island.

My landlord, Tommy Wordsworth, was a twenty-seven-year old, who also had been to my school. How he managed to have a house I do not know. I think his parents had separated when he was still at school and he got the house as compensation, or just somewhere to live.

He lived in the front room downstairs, a horrid mess full of the usual piles of hi-fi equipment and sleeping bags. Every once in a while his father came to stay in one of the rooms. He was a printer who worked at Fleet Street, but was now moved to Wapping, a miserable, taciturn man who showed no joy in anything, as far as anyone could see it. He was oozing bloody-mindedness, never even looked at you but expressed contempt with the angle of his head and the impatient way he breathed.

You could hear him barking out a few terse sentences to his son, and you knew why his son, Tommy, was a nervous and defensive young man who struck a posture of being callous. Tommy was also a strangely sensitive boy, he was good-looking, with a watery face, but he expressed weakness. He tried to talk crudely about girls to impress us but we only felt repelled, he seemed pitiable. Tommy tried to rip you off at every turn, a few pence here a few pounds there. He had learned to look after himself and he knew the value of money.

There was a young couple who had the big room upstairs at the front, they were only a couple of years older than me but he had a job in a garage and she had a job too, only she did night classes as well, and wanted to be a designer. They were working class, from Brimsdown, the other side of Enfield. We got along really well, visited each other's rooms, swap-borrowed records, I gave them Dylan and they gave me Talking Heads. We treated each other with respect and consideration. They slept early as they had to get up for work. I slept late, we shared the kitchen and she kept it nice. I was really fond of them.

One day they had a big row and she left slamming the door behind her, and Colin drank nearly a whole bottle of whiskey and nearly died. I found him by the front door and had to call an ambulance. He came back two days later and so did she, and we went back to normal. You used to be able to hear them making love all the way down the corridor and down the stairs to my room, she moaned and moaned and it gave the house a pleasant, peaceful, happy atmosphere.

In my room I read *A Portrait Of The Artist As A Young Man* by James Joyce, as well as the early version of the same book, called *Stephen Hero*, which concentrated on the two years around the same age as I was then. Being from an Irish Catholic background myself I felt as if I was reading up on my own childhood and a sort of lost life or lost self; the family and relations he had, I had too, the Sunday dinners, the details of life. His was more formal and clever than mine and so it seemed to complete a missing aspect of my life as I had lived it in my entirely bookless home where Guinness and beer eventually replaced the Catechism and even replaced hose-racing itself, which had been the nearest to literature we had. I did self-portraits of myself looking even more Irish than my looks already showed me to be. I read the nine hundred pages of *Ulysses*. I ate breakfast in cafés and bought strong beer and smoked and read more Irish pages until I felt as if I had caught up with myself.

In the meantime Lotta's letters came almost every day and I wrote mine too at the same rate. I had one passport-sized photograph of her, with luminous skin, hair brown and gold that curled in rings even though it was really just straight hair, and glasses, she almost always wore glasses, round, gold ones. Her lips were broad and perfectly shaped and full, her eyes were bright, bright blue, and her nose was delicate and pointed upwards. It was easily the most beautiful face I had ever seen or have ever seen since. It was the kind of face men stared at but didn't know what to do about. It gave you a sense of responsibility. I kept the photo in my breast pocket and rationed myself looking at it.

Some evenings I went on the tube-train to Earls Court, to the Troubadour Café where poets read their poetry out to an audience. I read mine, and because I was still the youngest there, I had been going there off and on since I was sixteen, I did pretty well and was always applauded generously and felt as if they listened with some sort of tension to see if I would manage to read something that actually sounded like a poem, and I did because mine were more immediate than theirs were, and my reading voice hadn't assumed that strange, dead 'poetry voice,' that they had, each one of them. I just read it like spoken words and it was like electricity in those small basement rooms.

It was exciting even though London seemed then as if nothing whatsoever was ever going to happen on a Wednesday evening, even at the famous Troubadour.

One night I met a man who pretended to be Michael McClure, and another night I actually met Dominic Behan who had written *The Patriot Game* and *McAlpine's Fusiliers,* two songs I knew by heart. I wanted to sing the last one to him, but sadly he said he already knew it. I bet he had forgotten the lyrics though, judging by the wry look on his face.

There were other poetry groups where people sat round in circles in community centres, like self-help groups, or like in a prison- very depressing; and very bad poetry.

No matter where I was, the best bit was always being allowed to get out and leave, to go back into the cavernous London Underground which to me then was like a nightmare or dream environment, sinister and foreboding, architectural structures that filled my unconscious, and I dreamt them for years afterwards.

They weren't utilitarian, they were phantasmagoric, bigger and more desperate than modern man could construct – I knew they had been made centuries ago when men of genius worked their wonders; long empty walkways, not neatly ending in plastic cladding but fading away into iron or stone caves and stores and tunnels where nobody knew where they ended up. London in those days was a place where anything like poetry or art was definitely a sideline, a dead end, not the multi-million pound art and culture industry it is today.

January was ending and my mind was drifting to the north. Our love letters were timidly groping their way forwards from our five meetings in London, towards a point where there was nothing more that you could dare to say until we met again. It had already been agreed that I would go to Sweden on the fourteenth of February in time for her half-term holiday called the 'sports holiday' when they are supposed to all go skiing.

I had no idea how long it took to get there, so I started thinking about leaving. I had a few hundred pounds my great-grandfather had left me, saved up from his twenty-five years as a stoker at the gasworks in Greenwich, followed by an astonishing thirty-five years on their pension. I had a small rectangular leather case, like the kind children keep dolls' clothes in, I had a black suit jacket and waist-coat and rings on my fingers and a pair of George boots I had found for seventy-five pence in Oxfam, and my father's overcoat from the 1960s which he used to wear when he worked up town. He too had worked in Fleet Street, like Tommy Wordsworth's father.

4

I took a train to Dover Western Docks where the ships nestled like boats in the bath under the great rock of the cliff, except that smoke curled up from their funnels, and Jubilee Way seemed like it had just been built - I remembered seeing it cutting through the cliffs as a child and hating it.

Ferry after ferry edged their way past the old harbour wall and out onto the rough sea. I had never been abroad before, only fishing in a boat with my father and the local butcher and an alcoholic dental technician from India, seven miles out into the channel, to where the look-out towers were built during the war and still remained, where we caught a five-foot congereel that chased me around the boat.

Within two hours I was standing in Calais, hitch-hiking. In those days the ferry left you off in the centre of town, and there I was. I had no idea how to do it, and it was night-fall before I was in Belgium.

One motorway is much like another, but these were eerily dowsed in mist that never ended. I had to get off them before my eyes burst from staring at the white, and I found myself in the middle of a bleak, cold countryside. I slept in a furrow of a foggy field, for an hour or so, alongside some cabbages left over from the previous year. They hadn't been harvested, they were rotting away, now frozen. It was icy cold and I only dozed. Unable to sleep properly I got up out of the ditch and walked into town. The town was Brugge, Bruges, where Van Eyck, the fifteenth-century painter, had lived.

I knew his work a little, I had worked at the National Gallery selling books and prints, and you could go into work early and have thirty minutes alongside some of the rarest, most valuable paintings in the country, and no-one bothered you. One day I ran into Sir Anthony Blunt, the famous spy who had been the Queen's art advisor; he was there having a private whisk-round view - and that was *after* he had been caught as a traitor. You could stand right up next to those paintings, even touch them if you wanted to, or smell them too, the smell filled the rooms, you could almost hear them in the silence before the gallery opened.

I found Van Eyck by the canal mixing pigment into warm linseed oil, but it was early morning and there was nothing and no-one, just mist, so I made my way out again and picked up an early lift in the pitch-black winter morning, about five o'clock.

A gnarled, hard-looking sailor driving a tiny Renault picked me up. He drove that Renault carelessly, as if he was driving it straight to the junk yard, the crushers' yard. He didn't speak much English but after a few minutes of silence he said, as we hurtled across the Belgian cement, in the only car on the road;

'Do you like sex?'

Miraculously there was a set of traffic lights in the wide empty road, and I got out and stood in the mist once again.

Another two hours of standing around in the freezing fog of the low countries. Rows of strange dwarf-like trees, black and distorted, lined the roads and the ditches and a thousand cattle lay sleeping, or glowering at the droplets in the air.

With daylight came traffic and a series of decent lifts got me into Germany, flying on Hitler's autobahn, built for speed and destruction. I saw the wreckage of a family, their caravan hit by a fast saloon like a tornado, children's toys strewn along the wide road.

Nightfall found me at a service station and the signs said that Hamburg was somewhere within striking distance. I didn't have a map and I wasn't quite sure where Hamburg lay except that it was somewhere on my path, towards Denmark. The signs told about kilometres and I wasn't sure how to convert them to miles.I bought myself a giant hamburger in honour of my next port of call, and ate it at a table in the comfort of the service station. My flagging strength was revived by the food, but it was night and I hadn't had any sleep to speak of except the nap with cabbages between two and three o'clock the previous night, and the night before that had been short in my eagerness to leave. My brain was hopping about and I was feeling twitchy and nervy. My ultimate destination was all that kept me from getting the creeps in the middle of Germany, sleepless and guideless.

I promised myself a bed in Hamburg, prised myself off the plastic sofa and went out into the dark to get a lift. Realising that I wouldn't probably get one at that time of night made me anxious in earnest. I couldn't keep my eyes open even when standing up and I was starting to feel strange, as if I was dreaming the German language that rattled around me, and dreaming the country I had only ever heard of, but which seemed to stretch out like a vast pool between me and the promised land.

I stood forlorn on the slip-road out of the service station. A plush car stopped and the driver offered me a lift, a German businessman in a suit, middle aged, prosperous, not the one you might have picked as likely to give a lift to a nineteen-year-old wandering male. He was friendly and interested. I felt I had to talk to pay my way, to provide some company. I told him my mission, he seemed to approve and it made him trust me;

'Swedish girls,' he said ' are the most beautiful in the world.' I'd heard that before, of course, I had almost forgotten it though, in recent months, their world-beating reputation was lost like a wave in the sea of Lotta's charismatic perfection; Swedish au-pairs I had known in print, the blonde pneumatics from *Mayfair* magazine or *Fiesta*, strewn around park flower-beds; Lotta had in fact told me she too had been an au-pair in London when she was seventeen. She had also worked as a librarian in an English sea-side town for a few months. I told all this to my businessman friend, it seemed like the kind of thing he wanted to hear, as he sped at diabolic speed past Hamburg and beyond, into Denmark.

My consciousness mixed my tale with passing thoughts and I asked him if I might sleep and he kindly let me. He drove on, past Kiel and Flensburg and into Denmark, where I awoke at four in the morning, and we parted. I was now in Scandinavia.

The sleep in the Mercedes hadn't been enough to clear my brain, which seemed now to be passing in and out of sleep without any control over it on my part.

I found myself on foot approaching a tiny quayside. Next to it was the rear end of a tiny ferry, like a sort of drive-on car ferry that would maybe take one or two cars. Beyond the ferry was a lake or a sea, I couldn't tell. The ferry began to move off. Without thinking, I ran, I sprinted and leapt from the quay to the tail of the ferry...

I made it. I was lucky to be alive. I can't even swim. It was like a leap from the real into the unreal, from the big, leaden grey world I had come from, to the smaller painted world of make-believe I was going to. I think as I sailed through the air in my leap, I left behind the normal probability and limitation of a boy from London for the freedom and colour of the fairy tale.

Maybe I did die, maybe my foot slipped on the quay as I was to slip in the snow many times thereafter, and I died in the freezing, foaming water churned up by the ferry; I died and my spirit soared on, and landed on a boat that was too small to be real, it could only be made up by Hans Christian Andersen. It would be the fitting transformation required for me to be able to live the rest of my life with a creature that I had already judged to be more like an invented fairy than a human.

The body and mind that slumped in the plastic chair on the ferry and fell into a coma-like sleep were real and the sleep was like a hostile wall that fell upon me and wouldn't let me stand or even open my eyes. I travelled back and forwards I don't know how many times, presumably three times, as finally I ended up on the right side of the water, after one time ending up back where I had started. I was almost in good enough condition to continue my journey. I was getting desperate but I was also getting closer. I decided to make it to Copenhagen then take a train to Sweden, and Stockholm, from there.

Many hungry, tired hours later I finally arrived in Copenhagen and gratefully booked my ticket on a Sweden-bound night train. The way at last lay open to me. I would get there, without a doubt. All I had to do was to get on that train and sleep and I would wake up in Stockholm.

There was already a bit of snow on the ground in Copenhagen and the buildings were an alien version of our own redbrick, with their pretty gables, and I glimpsed the green copper roofs with domes and spires. Their language sounded like English being spoken backwards, or like someone talking with hot soup in their mouth. Around the central station I saw small blond men in wooden shoes who looked like trolls. I also saw the races from Greenland who looked like American Indians I had seen in films, in Westerns, small and dark, red skinned, clutching bottles of fire-water. They had plaited hair, long and thick, nearly as black as my own. In the small supermarket in the station was a whole range of things quite unlike our own, crazy-looking names and sounds on milk packets, not bottles, paper cartons for everything and boxes of yoghurt with the yellow sun against a green background, painted on them.

The girls in the shops all were blonde and they looked right through you. They didn't smile or say hello like English girls, and they weren't as pretty, if you looked past the yellow hair. But they were inspiring because they looked all the same – I had at least arrived somewhere very particular. I was impatient to get to Sweden though and Denmark felt only like a halfway house, a foretaste, a lesser thing, still tasting slightly of Germany. I somehow knew Sweden was going to be unlike them all.

I was pleased to find that the train itself was Swedish. My heart raced at the sight of the Swedish names and words, the pale blue signs with white writing in a modern font, and the distinctive ö, ä and å letters that I had seen on Lotta's address, and on the stamps.

The very handles on the train doors were unlike the rest of the world's handles; expensive and elaborate, well-made hooks and catches, bold and clear. The wood which the interior was made of was deep reddish brown, and new, and it all had a sense of purpose that ran though every bolt and screw.

It was a whole world away from our own decay and cheapening and loss of confidence and the slow, self-hating vandalism of our nation that no longer believed in itself, our organised, passive, abject self-destruction. This Sweden was a country on top of its game, it was expensive. I stared at the place-names on the boards that were slotted into holders on the sides of the train, so bold and blue. I was elated to find that the mythical land that had invented Lotta actually existed and was so robustly itself; its unreal spirit clashed dramatically with the heavy reality of a train. The brick-red locomotive stood luxurious and self-assured, out on the platform alongside the dowdy Danish trains.

The night-train had compartments and I slid open the heavy door to mine. I knew it was mine because you had to make a seat reservation as well as buy a ticket, and that had cost almost as much. It was all highly organised, hard and cold with no room for mistakes. The Swedes don't need you and they expect the same in return.

I had been allotted to share my compartment with only one

other. This was good because it meant we could each spread our legs out on the seats alongside us and eventually sleep in comfort.

My travelling companion greeted me as I came in. He wasn't Swedish, he was Finnish. He looked like no-one I had ever seen before, at least people didn't look like that in my part of the world, not any more, if they ever had done. He had long blonde hair and a long beard, his hair was tied in a braid or something and his clothes were of the unconventional convention I had already noticed in Copenhagen. A soft, artistic look you could never have got away with in London, not if you wanted people to take you seriously. We were too knowing and funny for that. He was indeed a painter and talked about it without any of the self-consciousness born of that cynicism we have in England. For better or for worse he was just without it, he had no-one looking over his shoulder as he spoke.

I felt like I was going back into the nineteenth century, to a younger world where you could still believe in something, in what you were doing. It was inspiring, uplifting.

Here was someone who knew what he was and was serious about it and had no doubts. He was also a grown-up, and had already found his way in the world. I was still a child, and nothing I could say yet about anything could mean all that much. But for the first time in my life I was talking to someone for whom art and writing actually was part of the real social and political world.

Not even at the Troubadour had I found that. That was an island. This was an induction into a different world, one that was at once more naïve and wiser, less corrupted and degraded, but sometimes unable to tell the difference between fake and real.

I was to experience that dichotomy in my relations with Sweden for years, and it would never be fully resolved. It didn't really suit me or my temperament or mentality. But that night was a revelation and a relief. It was exciting to be allowed into a world, any world, where the words could be used simply; it was a place where things were more possible, where positions and identities hadn't all been used up, rejected and discredited. I regret that I couldn't have dived into it fully and taken advantage of that openness and freshness, I knew that already. I was nevertheless excited to be talking about philosophy and art with this grown-up on the eve of my arrival in my longed for destination. Any other night it would have been a thrill; this night it was like an alternative destiny.

Minutes after we left Copenhagen we were on a fifteen-minute ferry across the Sound, the narrow stretch of water between Denmark and Sweden, and no sooner had the clunking of the chains fastening the train to the deck stopped, than it began again... we were in Sweden.

I looked out of the window, the train was still on the ferry and I saw my first Swedish man, he was loosening the chains. He called out in the course of his work, so I heard Swedish for the first time, from a ferryman with chains. It was a language I would eventually learn fluently, but here I was hearing its pure sound alone, no meaning. It was clearer and, rounder than Danish, not clogged up but rhythmic and bright. The man was tall, big-boned and blonde, and as I looked about, scanning every person I saw on the boat and on the quayside as we trundled off the boat, this look was the norm. It struck me that this was the physical context of Lotta, and that compared to her countrymen and women she was small and a bit darker-haired, although essentially light-toned as they all seemed to be. I thought of her moving around amongst these giants, and that her life had so far been played out here among them. I thought of them having her here, seeing her.

Suddenly the train was on land, and seemed to be sitting in the middle of a small town square. The harbour merged with the streets, the train was next to the shops, all closed now. A small, pretty, red-brick station building was a few yards away. The whole place was covered in snow, snow like I had never seen before, snow that didn't look like it was going anywhere for a long time.

'I forgot to tell you we passed Hamlet's castle on the Danish side as we left the port,' said my companion. But I had seen it, without knowing whose it was; a vast series of towers and green spires. It wasn't a military castle like ours mostly are. I had toured on foot the castles in Wales, two years before, Caernavon and Harlech, castles with skirt walls so thick you couldn't doubt their purpose. Hamlet's castle wasn't any good for that. It sat prettily enough on a rock outside Elsinor (Helsingör), and it looked already in my mind then like a place for princes to wonder why or if, and for princesses to fall from walls.

The train pulled out from Helsingborg and we entered the tunnel of snow and night that began a few feet from the window, like a never-ending igloo arched over the train that wormed its way forward hundreds of miles. My companion told me that beyond the light of the train windows, it really was as dark as it looked, and that the Swedish forest was to all intents endless, that if you went into it you needn't come out again until you reached the Arctic circle one thousand miles away. My mind boggled, I was hoping the train wouldn't break down.

It didn't break down. It rang its bells through scores of level crossings, the slow certain bell of the long distance train, like I'd heard in American films, the rugged persistence of the rails traversing the un-traversable. And the music of its progress was punctuated by the guard who sang a spoken song about the next station as it approached, walking the length of the train; 'Alvesta nästa' or 'Linköping nästa,' I can still hear it now as it sounded to me then, the slow rhythmic voice of those Swedish guards, sleep walking. It was a bright blue world of perfection, being inside it was like being in a celluloid fiction and my painter friend was played by James Stewart and I was the little old Irish fairy.

Sweden seemed as everyone tended to think, 'modern,' its face set towards the future. It had clearly embraced something whole-heartedly, I just couldn't tell what quite yet. But it was also old-fashioned, something of its recent past had been preserved, you can't get away from all those trees that easily or quickly and no-one wanted to. Many of the houses are made of wood, and they keep the cold out, backed up by several nuclear power stations generating more electricity than a country four times its size would need. They left nothing to chance in their battle against nature. You got the feeling that the battle must have cost them dearly over hundreds of years, kept them poor and kept them dead and abject, and now final victory belonged to modern man, and Swedes drove that victory home without mercy. Everything worked, and making everything work was now a way of life, nothing else mattered, you didn't matter.

I could hardly contain my happiness or excitement; this was her country, I was deep inside it, enveloped by its inscrutable singularity. Every glance of every street I could catch from the window as the train threw itself through the towns, showed the unfolding picture of how alien she was. And yet, however perfect and self-contained this land seemed to be, I realised with each glance that she was strange within it, that the other-worldliness of her was not yet explained even by this remarkable place. Maybe the key to it was that while this place made it *possible* to belong to some archaic mountain troll race, it didn't make it *necessary*. The place was full of normal people, I could see their cars parked, their shops, their pizzerias, hear them talking in the compartment next to ours, they were enchantingly foreign, but they were normal; she, I was realising, was something else.

Her identity drifted in and out of my mind, mixed with my conversation with Erkki Pirtola the Finnish painter, and the flashes of Sweden I was getting as we passed the lights, as well as from the tunnel of light our compartment created as we hurtled along. I was getting to know her better with every hour I travelled. I was sorting through my five actual meetings with her, the many letters I had received from her.

One such letter was a postcard, it was of a painting by the painter I now know as John Bauer, who lived at the turn of the century. It was a curious painting that made a strong impression on me when I got it, more than a postcard of a work of art might usually do. A shot of adrenalin ran though my arms when I saw it and still does now when I remember that alien item falling into my North London letter box at the beginning of my life when my senses were still awake and when the true nature of something could shoot like an iron rod into the mind and light everything up, and change perceptions in one second. It wasn't a card from a museum, it was a picture of the real thing, it was as real as if a mad creature had crept through the door and set up camp in the hallway.

It was a painting of a troll-child kneeling naked beside a pool, in a forest, its hair very long and falling down onto the ground past its knees covering it up. The forest receded into darkness in the background behind her; you could just see a few grey shapes of trees in the blackness. She is made brightly visible by a soft light that, no matter how soft it is, is an impossible light because neither the sun nor moon could ever penetrate though that forest. She is kneeling beside a pool of water as black as the forest beyond, aside from the light cast by her own reflection which she beholds, pulling her gold hair gently to one side as she does so. When I saw it I thought how lonely and magical Swedish art was and how full of the old folk tales things seemed to be there; even the stamps on her letters seemed to be referring to it.

But now when it came back to me there in the night train, I realised a flash of something that made my scalp tingle – that child was her.

I don't know what made me realise it, or think it. Then I asked myself; do I mean simply that she was intending the painting to represent her when she sent it, so that she was saying 'this is me,' or did my realisation mean that somehow that depicted creature in the painting was actually her? That would mean that when John Bauer painted it he was paining the very same creature as I had travelled across Europe to see, and would see, in only a few hours? The unreality of the thought escaped me, I couldn't judge it to be so, it seemed like a real question; I was drifting into sleep. Instead of falling asleep I asked Erkki if he knew of such a painting. Of course he did, I hadn't realised how well known it was.

'What is the creature on the painting?'

He explained that it could be a number of things;

'It could be one called Skogsrå, she lures simple labouring men into the forest at night, she is very beautiful, but when he has been riding her all night, and she turns away to leave, he sees that she has no back.'

'No back?' I asked dreamily.

'Yes, you know, just blood and bones. But really I think it isn't that, I think it is just a *troll barn*, a troll-child, the child of a troll. She sits in the road and pretends to be lost, then she goes home with the simple labourer, to his simple cottage and then makes him promise to marry her when she is old enough and he agrees because it seems so far away in time, and that way she gets him, because you can't break a promise to a troll-child for then her father pulls your head off.'

I laughed a sea of little waves of laughs because I hadn't slept for three days and that makes you see the comical side of everything. I pictured myself as a Swedish country labourer and Lotta as a troll, and laughed some more and floated off on the laugh, thinking that she wasn't a troll at all, she was that other one, the one with no back.

'Of course, most likely it's just a normal child looking at its reflection in the dark forest, you know.' said Erkki.

When I woke up we were pulling into Stockholm Central Station.

Erkki sat grinning at me. He was already awake and ready, his bag was off the rack and next to him on the seat.

'Don't worry, you have some few minutes left.'

Those few minutes later we stood in the middle of the Central Station. It's a big hall, no trains, the trains are on platforms away off through some doors. At the far end of the Art Deco hall, there was a raised balcony that looked like a café. It was relatively quiet for a central station of a big city, sedate and pretty, smaller than Copenhagen and tiny compared to London's stations. A likeable sort of place. We agreed to go and have some breakfast on the balcony, and that I should go and make my telephone call.

I knew Lotta was still at school, her holiday not yet begun, and that she wasn't expecting me, and she had probably left her home for school already, it being about half past nine in the morning. On our *second* meeting in London, as we danced a slow dance together, she had told me she lived in a tree house.

The 'tree house' turned out to be a wooden villa, a large house in a rich suburb (the Swedish word for *wood* being the same as that for *tree)*, owned by her grandparents or friends of her grandparents, I couldn't remember which, where she had a small apartment that she shared with a friend. I phoned her there and there was no answer. My next call was to her parents who were in a town thirty-five miles away. They would tell me

41

how I should get to her apartment. I dialled and said 'Hello' when it was answered.

A middle-class, male, English voice answered me. It was her father. His English was impeccable. The kind of voice that said 'necessary' in the old BBC way, 'necessry' not the slightly Americanised we say it in now.

He knew who I was, she must have told them of the impending visit of a young Englishman. He was very friendly and helpful. He told me that Lotta had gone to school by this time and that she would be back at half past four. He then described to me how to get to where she lived. It was quite complicated and daunting, but I wrote it down carefully. He sounded very posh to me, but apparently he was only a teacher.

I went back to Erkki. His train went at six o'clock so we agreed to spend the day together. He was good company, I was very pleased. He said he would take me to the Swedish National Gallery. I think he liked the idea of introducing someone to the unknown treasure.

And treasure it was. I could hardly believe it. My education, which had actually included A Level history of Art, was predictably narrow, and like most people I knew about French Impressionism and that in some detail.

Nowhere had it been mentioned that, as far as painting light was concerned, it had been done with more imposing effect in the North, where light really meant something else to them than what it meant to the French Impressionists. In France it was the embodiment of sight, of all you see. The old non-secret they re-discovered was that everything you see is just light, and if you want to paint what you see you must paint the light, and light is full of colours.

But in Sweden and Finland in the north, light wasn't this ocular phenomenon, it was the difference between life and death, happiness and misery, warmth and cold, hope and black despair. Light was in pretty short supply in the winter and although it was correspondingly plentiful in the summer that just wasn't enough to wipe out the memory of the months of cold and darkness, and the certainty that they would return.

It was therefore in the paintings of summer, of the long days of light when the sun almost never goes down (depending how far north you are) that their feelings about light reach the height of their intensity and also ambiguity. You could see it, you could see that no matter how long that light lasted, no matter how it left its unearthly blessing on the land or on a face or on a lake, the knowledge of its certain withdrawal made for sadness. The light couldn't take that sadness away. Their lives were hard too; the light dressed and described the beauty of the land, of the flowers, of the people, but the people were on a tightrope across fatal water. Anything could push them in. A bad harvest, a dead cow, an especially hard winter, could drive even the children to their graves. Sweden before the modern era had no robustness or security, didn't have the careless joy of the sweltering sun of the French South or the urbanity of Paris; it had a struggle to stay alive. Beauty had a cruelty in those circumstances.

So when the Nordic painters depicted light they were showing everything else too. They painted carefully, as if only by capturing the very precise flicker of late, soft rays on the water of the lake, could they convey the thought, the moment of doubt and secret suspicion of woe that it gives them. Their paintings had an accuracy and poignancy that made their French counterparts' work look like decoration.

The French paintings were about *painting*, and maybe that's why the modern era, obsessed as it is with 'art,' is so endlessly fascinated by it. Swedish paintings were about life, and not life as it is lived there now, but as it was lived some time ago, and as it is lived in many other places right now. It is not a painfulness we long to be reminded of. 'Art,' for us has greater possibilities. Erkki was passionately a Northerner, and knew all this of course partly from the activity of the light. He regarded French painting as I regard the Bossa Nova.

On that day in the National Gallery of Sweden, I learned about lakes and evening light and still, silent faces, of beautiful young women made old before their time with cares.

Looking at all that late evening summer light all day - suddenly the sun was gone! The sun went down at around half past two, disappeared in a sudden, short burst of hollow blue. They even have an expression for it, for the light departing the snow, the Blue Hour. Erkki and I had lunch and then I felt excitement and desire seeping into my head like spilled wine across a table cloth, and I realised that the actual hour I had been anticipating for so long was nearly upon me. In one hour's time I would see Lotta, her actual self, while I had been only dreaming about the image of her left in my memory, for weeks. She might even be finishing school now, this very moment.

Erkki pointed me to the right underground station and helped with directions and wished me good luck with my journey and my life and I thanked him for a great introduction to

Swedish painting and off I went.

Night and snow awaited me as the underground shot me out at my station where I was to find a bus. The bus took me across a bridge to the island where Lotta's suburb, Lidingö, was to be found. I got off too early, afraid to be whisked away into the dark unknown. It was the wrong stop and so I didn't really have directions any more. I wandered off in the dark and snow in search of the house I had seen in the little photograph she had shown me.

I ended up on some ice that was in fact the sea that surrounded the island. I had never walked upon ice before, never walked upon the sea. It was terrifying to go out towards the blackness, the great well of the unconscious that is the sea, to walk into it, upon it, supported only by a thin crisp of ice, God knew only how thick or how thin, I certainly didn't. What compelled me to walk on it I didn't know. I retreated after forty yards or so, and felt the devil at my back like you do as a small child fleeing down a dark staircase.

On land again, I realised I was lost, no-one around to ask. I did enjoy being part of a Swedish suburban weekday evening, dinners cooking inside the wooden villas that lined the road I walked down, a sparsely populated road.

Men were arriving home from work, I guessed, here as anywhere else, a real country with real people. Gables and fancy carpentry, houses from the 1900s and the 1920s, German-looking to me then in my ignorance, not English. A wealthy suburb: picturesque, ice, sea, boats frozen into the ice, their lonely flagpole ropes flapping and clanking in the winter breeze. It looked like a mountain of black water had fallen down upon the summer boat landscape and that everyone had scurried inside to hide and wait. The few people I saw on the road just walked past, no-one looked at me, they don't look at you like they do in England. If they can ignore you they will. I was on my own.

Finally too much time had passed so I knocked on a door and was given directions but no encouragement from the householders.

At last, there it was. A large house set back off the road on a slope. A big wooden villa, from 1915 maybe. A classy sort of house that was for sure. I wondered if she was there inside it. Could it really be the one?

I pushed open a small iron garden gate and went up the sloping path through the slippery snow. It had been shovelled recently but not today, some snow had filled the path up again. My unsuitable London boots slipped and slid on the solid-packed snow as they had all day. I could hardly keep my feet, going up that path. Lights were on but it was a three story house and dark at the top. Large granite steps went up to the front entrance. Something told me she wasn't going to be the one answering that door.

I rang, an old fashioned bell-pull like in the olden times. Ages later, as if no-one was ever expected to ring on the bell, I heard footsteps approaching. I could literally tell from them that an uninvited visitor was an annoyance. That was expressed in the approaching footsteps, somehow.

A tall, thin, grey-haired man opened the door and looked down at me from the light to where I stood down the steps, a small dark-haired young man with no hat (I did have a hat but it was in my hand). The man didn't say anything. I excused, apologised, I suddenly realised that there was a language problem – to suddenly be on an elderly Swedish gentleman's doorstep and speak English at him felt odd.

I asked for Lotta. He said she wasn't there. I quickly swallowed my amazement that this was the right place, and continued. I explained that I was supposed to be staying there, and could I come in and wait for her. I was worried about standing out in the minus ten cold for hours. What if she was out all evening?

The reluctant gentleman let me inside, he silently led the way. Had he understood me? He said so little. The house was very rich, this wasn't Socialist Sweden. Antique furniture all around, a wide staircase with portraits on the wall going up it. He led me past an open sort of living room, my eyes were going everywhere; past him, inside the room, was a woman in a wheelchair, his wife I guessed. He walked slowly up ahead of me.

Were these her grandparents or who were they? They didn't seem to know her all that well. My Lotta was a small creature, *that* sort of ex-au pair, a thin, harmless-looking vegetarian with round John Lennon glasses. Could she be the same Lotta who lived in a giant villa with an aristocratic landlord? Apparently.

We reached the top of the stairs ascending through the dark house. He knocked on the door to the flat, just a normal interior room door, although it was somehow clear that no-one was there, then he showed me in. The flat was essentially the top floor of the house. He opened another small door, and turned on the light and said;

'You must wait here,' and left me. I couldn't help feeling that he left me in dismay or disgust. He couldn't relate to me at all, hadn't looked at me once, it was as if I wasn't there. Anyway I was alone now.

I was in Lotta's room.

5

I had to catch my breath and it wasn't because of the stately ascent of the Gothic staircase. I was at last in her room. Even though she wasn't there, she would be soon – I could see her, sense her, of course. The fact that she had recently been in the room gave it all the charisma it needed. I wasn't even surprised that the room was beautiful. It was a modestly sized room but everything in it was pretty - painted wood table and chairs, painted wooden bed that looked like an antique, delicately picked out in gold paint, in the fluting of its columns. At the far side of the room were three windows, arched, with a balcony beyond. The room was quite untidy.

I stood totally still, like when you find yourself inside a church with a hammer-beam roof. Her knickers were on the floor. I had never seen her knickers, of course, so I felt that I didn't have the right to look at them now, so I looked away but I was constantly aware of their presence. I went and sat at her desk and tried to be as decorous as possible.

I told myself I was in a young lady's bedroom, unexpected, sort of uninvited, she didn't know I was going to be let into her room and didn't know I was coming today. I was about two weeks early. My hitch-hiking had been too quick. I suddenly worried that I might not be convenient at all. It might be inconvenient, it might be - my eyes went to her knickers. They were pink cotton. I looked away and resolved not to look again. My heart was racing. I was here, right there in her room. That such a place existed, a room that was hers, anywhere on earth, was remarkable to me then, and I had found my way to it, crawled across Europe to find it hidden in the dark.

She was there in the doorway.

A big smile. Such a warm, loving face. She was glowing, it was a historical moment, there at the beginning of our lives. She stood still in the doorway, shy and grinning and glowing. The cold of the snow still hung about her. We looked at each other across that room, our lives entwining there and then, centuries falling away, like the ice that forms and then falls away from the space-rocket as it takes off on its way to the mad moon, great giant flakes of new-formed ice made by the intense heat of the fuel, a crazy crashing of sheets of ice in darkness falling.

She put her bag down and came and sat on my knee. She sat astride me, legs either side of me, and put her arms around my neck and looked directly into my face. She smelt of fresh air. Such a sexual position can only be explained by the fact that we had never ever sat like that before, and sex was no part of our five times together, except kissing, and this was romance and love. We had been in love since the first time we met. Any sex that came into the moment through the way she chose to sit on me, came like a guest invited to sit and wait in the corner;

Do come in and wait, we will be hearing a lot from you later no doubt, we hadn't even planned for your visit but we will drink a furtive tea with you at night.' So, sex waited, sat in the corner, sat on our laps and on her thighs, and waited quietly.

We kissed modestly, pleasantly, a greeting on pursed lips. She smiled some more at me and sat some more with her legs. And then she said, as if she had been rehearsing for the arrival of her English guest;

'Would you like a cup of tea?' in her very best English. And with racing heart, so full of contentedness and happiness and at such hearts-ease, I followed her to the kitchen. It must have been about half past five in the afternoon, but if felt like three in the morning.

We sat in the kitchen and drank tea and I ate cheese for the first time in my life, with cheap, red, Swedish caviar from a tube. We talked of nothing. We had nothing to talk about, we didn't know anything about each other, except that we were in love.

We talked about the objects in front of us, our tea cups, her table. I don't think we talked of my journey, it had nothing to do with being there, now with her. The road that lay behind me held no interest for me, and she was not bold enough to be curious. I stared at her, astonished at every detail that confirmed her existence, a sock, a corduroy knee, a bowl of sugar, her actual face that now at last glowed before me, the face whose image I had rationed to myself, now was here for me to look at constantly.

I haven't taken my eyes off that face since, one way or another.

My head was swimming after a few days without proper sleep, and I might as well have been dead and with the world of souls for all I cared, I was there with the fairest creature on

God's earth, and I knew then that I would never really want to be anywhere else ever again, and would have to drag myself round this old world, from this place to that, trying to pursue any destiny that wasn't written on her face.

She wasn't witty, she had no opinions, she didn't even talk very much, she was the gatekeeper of a secret world. The normal universe, the rest of it, seemed so far away, and distances seemed further than ever. I would have swapped the rest of my life to stay in that kitchen with her forever. It was like I had been told that I was a millionaire; I wanted to sit spending that first ten pounds, I had no need to spend the rest, not yet anyway.

At around eleven o'clock, Lotta announced that it was time for bed and within a few tooth-brushing minutes we were in her room. She pointed to a small spare bed alongside her own and said;

'You can sleep there, Or you can sleep in my bed with me.'

Seeing as how we hardly knew each other it was a fair question, but there was really not much of a choice to be made for any mortal being. Our relationship had been so much about love, that her suggestion that I slept with her seemed almost shocking; no, it *did* seem shocking. Despite her very obvious charms, sex was not in the air, just the rays of romance like from a renaissance sun. We were getting married, we were heading for an altar, with or without vicar or priest, maybe a pagan altar, but an altar. In fact her white and gold painted bed looked like a pagan chariot, or like the chariot of the twins in the Tarot pack.

I looked at it and wondered where on earth it came from. Was it hers? Did she take it around with her wherever she went.

Surely it can't belong to that long thin grey-haired aristocratic doorman downstairs? It was the effort of thinking of the bed belonging to that man, and the sheer impossibility of it, that made me realise that the bed, as well as being expensive, antique and extravagantly peculiar, was strangely obscene, if a bed can be obscene by itself. Maybe it really was an altar? My mind was frying, the hours and days of no sleep were unlocking caverns of my unconscious and releasing their perspicacity. I was seeing things as they really are, and that can only be followed by oblivion.

Anyway, the real me was just a simple Catholic boy, I'd led a sheltered life, not abnormally so, but anyway. It seemed that, if it weren't for this bed question we would drift slowly into the right activity at the right pace, pretty quickly. Suddenly she had an, alien to me, Scandinavian, business-like air, a no-nonsense, straightforward manner, not so much erotic as modern. I wondered if she was terribly sophisticated despite her child-like exterior. Naturally I opted for the sharing-her-bed option and within a very few minutes in that bed she announced;

'This is getting a bit dangerous."

She said we had to stop until we would get condoms tomorrow.

I hadn't thought of condoms or anything like that. In fact I was relieved that she thought I was doing well enough for the matter to arise. I thought we were only kissing and fumbling around. She seemed to mean that kissing in a bed meant sex all the way, straight away, every time.

She slept with her head on my chest and looked like an angel torn down from the sky. Her delicate up-turned nose and her perfect mouth I just stared at until I too fell asleep, to the sound of choirs of angels. No doubt they were looking down upon her from the ceiling, to see she didn't go astray.

When I awoke the next morning she was over by the window in her night dress, talking on the phone. I had never heard her speak her own language before and I was very interested to hear it. Her mouth moved in a different way to make the different sounds. There were new sounds, a kind of shshshing, and unaspirated sucking and blowing noises delicately executed by teeth and lips.

The singsong, up and down thing you always heard in sitcoms, when there were tall Swedish girls with big breasts and yellow hair, was completely lacking, but then Lotta was shorter and darker, despite having been an au-pair and fitting the clichés in every other way, to my schoolboy satisfaction.

I was in a light mood, watching her there. All my life, since I was five years old, I had dreamed of European women and airports. God knows where I got the idea from then, I think we picked up my aunt from Heathrow, from a flight from Holland in the fog.

That might have been where it started, or like any lower-class English boy brought up on television, I wanted a Swedish girl, they were legendary, and this was grafted onto my airport fantasy. Idyllic love and Destiny was one thing, fulfilling your teenage fantasies was another, and I had managed both in one sudden movement, before life had really started.

Lotta looked more animated and confident talking on the phone than I had seen her; she had always seemed controlled and contained, painfully shy as they say, awkward and un-spon-taneous – each movement had seemed as if it had been invented

54

as a stop gap until the conventional ones could be located.

I had never seen or met anyone so awkward or tense, it was nerve-wracking to watch her, each moment was fraught and its difficulty registered on her face, on her mouth and in her eyes as immobility. Her aim was to show as little on her face as possible, to react as little as possible, to anything. Apart from that, she was like a child, in other words, like herself a few years ago. She smelt of apples, if of anything at all, she left no trace, she was made of paper. When she was in a room your eyes were upon her, nothing you were doing before could compete with watching her move about the room. She didn't talk much but was as warm and friendly as anyone could be. She grinned like the Cheshire cat, had the same mouth full of teeth, and most of the time kept her mouth shut. She was even the motherly type, you knew if you went on a trip somewhere she'd take a picnic, and help you if you were ill or down. You felt so safe with her, in her company, why would you ever want to leave it? I wondered, even though she was so young, how she could be still available. She conveyed most of her personality with her eyes or by some other means, indirectly, because it wasn't with words.

She finished on the phone and said;

'I'm not going to school today, shall we go to Stockholm?'

Stockholm is built on a series of half-islands. The buildings date mainly from the 1890s onwards and are long four or five storey apartment blocks, often mustard coloured, but they can be wine red or white or grey too. When I saw them that winter, icicles had formed on the edges of the roofs, maybe five storeys up and men were employed to knock those icicles down before they plummeted to the pavement and killed someone.

She guided me along the streets, a real town, a real city, concentrated, not spread out. Buses seemed to thrive on the ice and swooshed about gracefully and ruthlessly, and made a point of stopping inches from the kerb every time; you took your chances as a pedestrian, buses changed course for no-one, but everyone seemed to know that, so no-one was killed. Conditions, it seemed, had made them hard and ruthless in all but their strong belief in equality – but God help you if, despite it, you failed to be equal.

Lotta took me to a café. It was very old fashioned, it looked like something from the 1950s. It was dark and plain in its design. Men in some sort of uniform sat at dark wooden tables eating their lunches; they were taxi drivers. On the wall was a mural from the 1930s, of workers marching, like a Russian poster. A round woman came to take our order. Her Swedish sounded more like the Swedish I had expected to hear, an up and down rhythm. It must be some sort of dialect. Lotta seemed to be a regular there. I got pea and ham soup, home made, with yellow chick-peas and bits of pork in it, and three rolls, one cheese, one liver paté and gherkins, and one ham, on sweetened brown bread, syrup in the flour. And coffee. You could take as much coffee as you wanted. This was a long way from the crispbread and bicycles image of Sweden the advertising world had presented us with in England. That seemed to be middle-class Swedes . This was a working man's cafe and looked more like eastern Europe. I felt relieved we were going to eat proper food. Lotta was a vegetarian and I was beginning to wonder if I would ever see meat again. No-one looked at us while we were there. No-one seemed to look at anyone or speak to anyone they didn't know, in Sweden. I had already noticed it and it was confirmed everywhere I went.

From there we went to another café. This girl, moderately skinny though she was, consumed great quantities of cakes and sandwiches all day. She should have been fat. This next café was a different kind altogether, genteel, like a bourgeois living room from the 1890s, and on four floors. Tables with white linen cloths sagged under piles of cups and plates and heaps of cakes that made you weak at the knees just to look at them. The whole place was filled with the smell of coffee and of cream. You paid your money and sat on a sofa or in an arm chair and partook of the cakes. You could also have a chaise longue and sandwich (one layer of bread only, so not a sandwich really). Lotta put away another few of these and then got to work on the cream cakes. I was, as I have said, already in love with her and had been since the moment I saw her in London, but I was thinking, how could you not love someone who could eat that much cream cake and still look hungry and underfed? She worked hard at her figure and hardly had time to drink more than a couple of cups of coffee. I drank half of one cup and it gave me a cold sweat and the shakes.

'What in the name of God is this stuff?' I asked
'It's a bit strong,' she said, 'are you all right?' She told me that her parents both drink six cups each morning, to aid their digestion. I asked if they were in the land of the living, even though I knew they were. She said;

' We can go and find out because it is the weekend tomorrow, and I often go there at weekends,' then as if remembering something; 'We must go late at night' she said 'I have to work.' I reassured her that I could wait to meet her parents if she had to work, that was fine. She walked over to the cake pile, word-less but taking my attention with her. She seemed put out by not being able to take me to her parents earlier. I wondered if it was a tradition. When she came back she asked if the journey to Sweden was very quick and easy. I said it was quicker than I thought.

'Did you really hitch-hike like you said you would?'

'Yes but it took only three days and I thought it would take a week or so, I'm not very good at geography.'.'

'It's so good you came soon,' she said.

'I thought I was going to be a few days early but I'm ten days early, aren't I?'

'Yes ten days exactly,' she laughed and ate a cake; I haven't made arrangements' she said, through cream.

'Oh.'

'But it's OK, but I have to work a little when I thought I wouldn't while you were here'

'Oh that's OK,' I said, 'for me I mean. But for you of course, it's....' I couldn't remember, I wasn't sure if it mattered or not, I could see she was someone who liked to be organised.

'What do you do? ' I asked.

'When?'

'When you work.'

'Oh I only work in a bar, nothing interesting.'

The sun was already going down, it was about three o'clock and the yellow sun's rays bobbed in through the window and said goodbye to her white, motionless cheek.

That afternoon, my very first day in Stockholm, she took me to a place called Waldermars Udde, the country home of a man called Prince Eugene, now an art gallery housing his collection. He had been a friend of Strindberg, the famous Swedish playwright, who was their national bard and a sort of conservative rebel at the same time, and a madman and alchemist to boot, as well as a painter. Prince Eugene was a painter himself. It was as if Lotta had conspired with Erkki to introduce me to Sweden by means of paintings, except that in her case it was a silent tour as she was not the type to comment upon what we were looking at, but she clearly took me there because it was a beautiful place on one of the islands of Stockholm, this one was surrounded by embassies, that has previously been the homes of the very rich.

'My great great aunt lived there,' she said as we went past one of the palaces set back off the road, 'Oh it's not a very big one,' she said as she noticed my astonishment, 'Look close.' So I did look close and indeed it was certainly one of the smallest mansions on the whole island, I guess there was no country small enough to want to have it as its embassy, for it was still a private home.

'Does she still live there? ' I asked

'Oh no.'

I pressed her on the family and got a relatively rambling answer which I couldn't follow, peopled with a string of notable and illustrious persons, bold and good and bad; one was the first female student, and patient, of Freud, another was the first female member of Parliament, another relative had been in prison in connection with a notorious accounting scandal and bankruptcy in which he was the accountant.

The other grandfather was an oil magnate and had founded Sweden's only oil company. Her grandmother had played with the king's brother as a child, for her father was a general. Her direct ancestor had been the second richest man in Sweden, in the 1790s in the days of iron ore. All the little red houses and cottages in Sweden that the world knows so well are painted with the red iron-oxide from these mines and foundries, the greatest of which was owned by her great-great-great-great-grandfather. Her parents were a mere librarian and a teacher.

'How low they have fallen,' I said as a sort of joke. She seemed surprised;

'I've never thought of it like that. They aren't very ambitious, it's true. I didn't think they could be anything else.' Her mind didn't seem to be on the conversation, something was troubling her.

' I think if we hurry we can get Fat Tuesday Buns at a café.'

Fat Tuesday Buns were a sort of cream cake that Swedes eat on Shrove Tuesday. They comprise a light bun, round with the top cut off, the middle of which has been scooped out and replaced with a soft pale yellow or white almond paste, not really marzipan but similar. On top of that is a large amount of whipped cream, and balanced on top of that is the lid of the bun, futile-looking and jauntily sailing on the solid sea of cream.

We got there just in time. Lotta ate two buns. I struggled with one. When she walked over to the coffee cups piled up on a table, it gave me another chance to look at her legs. I had not yet fully gauged what her appearance was despite being in bed with her. She didn't walk around under-dressed, you had to guess.

She habitually dressed like a vegetarian librarian, so nothing was very obvious. But, in a flash of moments between cream cakes, I saw confirmation of what I already suspected - the church mouse had killer legs.

Her legs, despite being thin and weak-looking at first glance, like the rest of her, were in fact perfectly shaped as far as the human eye could see. Her thighs, beneath the corduroy, were of the very first rank of thighs in the world. I was no expert, but they were screaming silently, 'We are part of the wide-world!.' They were world-class, even if their owner was a completely unknown nobody still in school, unwittingly accompanying world-beating legs around on her daily travels. It was a bit like discovering that someone, without realising it, was a concert pianist.

I had a feeling those legs were taking her unawares on a trip and deciding her destiny without even asking her. And it was all made out of cream, I don't think she had a muscle in her body.

She could certainly walk though, she was tireless. We had slid our way from one marvellous place to another in the gloom of the winter afternoon, fringed with red and a ghostly blue. The soles of my shoes were giving me problems and I had to cling onto her a lot of the time to avoid breaking my neck.

The reason I only glanced at her legs so briefly was that I could hardly take my eyes off her face. The atmosphere between us was light and friendly, she seemed pleased to be with someone who didn't irritate her. Her delight was visible when I made my replies and comments such as they were. I made a point of not saying too much or being too forceful. I got the impression she would be most pleased if only a person could avoid being tedious. Beneath our friendliness was the fact that we were in love, but we didn't mention it or refer to it even indirectly; romance hung around us like the garlands of great champions.

She was possessed of the warmest, friendliest eyes, and the wild beast within her that you fell in love with was almost entirely absent from them. Neither was there any place for lust, it was as if she didn't have a body. Love was all around her, you couldn't separate it from her, it clung to her as if it was clinging to a safe haven in a world where Love was looking for a home. Like a miasma, like a spirit, it formed up around her and sprang from her, her face shimmered because of it, you couldn't take your eyes off her. You wondered how she had got through life this far without being snatched away and melted down like a gold statue, or questioned and interrogated and made to explain, how she had got to be so. How *did* she get to be so? How could a normal life of schools and homes and streets and libraries and teachers produce a creature that is a focal point of the unknown.

This was the longest day we had ever spent together, and it had come after the night too. We had now spent as much time together as during the whole five meetings in London put together.

In Sweden, evening seemed to start at around five o'clock. It was dusk and everyone had gone home, the working day starts at around eight in the morning there, or even seven.

The heart of Stockholm was a frozen heart, the sea with ships in it, and three islands meeting at one point, the Royal Palace, the opera house, The Grand Hotel, a quay with icebreakers moored alongside it, small grey ships like tiny battleships to break the ice in the archipelago, little steamers too, from the 1890s, that August Strindberg's father had worked on, a low, flat centre of ice and beautiful buildings, and a cold wind blowing in off that ice.

We passed the National Theatre, a street with a giant mushroom in the centre of it from the 1930s, that led straight back from the present nuclear power state to the recent past where all the buildings and songs were from. She took me from one place to another as if she had an itinerary. She knew how her city could impress.

Suddenly we were down in the generously proportioned tunnels of the underground system; green trains that seemed to be from the 1950s, carved rock tunnels, recorded messages, bings and bongs, clean and bright, and whooosh – we were back at 'Shout-stone' (called so because, in the old days, you used to have to shout for the ferry to come and get you if you wanted to go to the island, her own island, Lidingö). Now there was a bridge, and a bus followed by a dark trudge took us back to the villa of the elderly landlord. The wife in the wheelchair waved to Lotta as we came in, a friendlier face. Lotta went and spoke to her and introduced me. I took her slight and elderly hand, and received her shaky smile.

We crept up the stairs to the upper floor and home.

'We can go and see my parents tonight,' she said with a contented grin, and flumped down onto the bed. 'You want to see where I grew up?'

I did, I wanted to see where she grew up, I wanted to see the parents who had helped her grow up.

I now got to meet her flatmate, who arrived just after we did. She was called Karin and was very pleasant and friendly and was a school friend of Lotta's. She was at university. She was the daughter of a judge and a teacher and was into politics and vegetarianism. She and Lotta were vegetarians together, in a cosy girls-together sort of a way, and Karin had a lot of posters on her wall about syndicalism and anarchism. Red and black are very attractive colours to people when it comes to politics.

It was all the usual left wing stuff but with a Swedish slant, so I learned a bit about recent Swedish history and politics, just from looking at Karin's wall.

Social Democracy had been the labour movement that had transformed Sweden from a harsh hierarchical society where the poor starved, into the most egalitarian in the world. Some form of serfdom was within living memory. Lotta and Karin were also in the campaign against nuclear power that was going on at the time; there was going to be a referendum on it.

They wore *Atomkraft Nej Tack* badges, I wore one too, and they used to go and eat soup with a group of older people who were also against nuclear power, and I guess they talked about it while they ate soup.

In the end the government split the *no* vote by inventing a third choice; 'No, but we dismantle nuclear power over the course of the next ten years.' That one actually won it, but of course ten years later it was a different government who didn't hold themselves bound by the referendum. The nuclear power programme of course wasn't ever dismantled, it was all just a lie and a scam to fool their own people. I guess the Swedish government thought they knew better the right course to take. There was no way they were going to let the people decide on such an important issue, so they stitched them up. It was obvious and shameless, but Swedes don't generally complain about their own government. Nowadays those soup-eating people, who were at this time against nuclear power, have turned into people who boast about Sweden's low emissions, because they rely seventy-five percent on nuclear power. They don't include nuclear waste in 'emissions' or pollution, despite its unlimited potential for destruction of the environment. This was anyway the soup-eating stage and it was a real issue that united left wing Swedes in their opposition to something.

We actually ate some vegetarian soup together and it seemed we all got along together well. I was OK at fitting in with girls, I didn't dominate the conversation or anything like that, as I had seen many young men do in the company of females, even when they're outnumbered. I had learnt to take a back seat and let the girls, who are generally more interesting talkers than boys, take the lead. I was thereby quickly accepted into the little ménage and we had a lot of fun together sitting around their table in the kitchen. There was an old chaise longue along the wall and, opposite that, a small built-in larder, a small electric cooker, then a window looking out to the other side of the house from Lotta's room. Tall pines were standing right up next to the house, one of them waved soberly at us through the window. We were going to sit there, all three of us, for many hours chatting and laughing. They had their own funny drink they wanted me to try, it was dreadful, they said, and laughed about it so much they could hardly say its name which was *surr* which was short for 'surrogate' but it also meant 'bitter' if you said it differently. It was a kind of ersatz coffee made of acorns or something. It was pretty foul. They drank it every day, just for laughs it seemed – so I joined them.

After soup, followed by endless cups of *surr* and open 'sandwiches' of cold cheese on toast with cheap red caviar and cucumber, Lotta suddenly announced that she had to go. I had forgotten she was going to work and so late. It must have been about half past nine already. I guessed it was a pretty late bar.

She disappeared off into her room then came back ten minutes later with her coat on ready to go.

She gave me instructions where and when to come and meet her – we were going to her home town that night, to see her parents, by the night bus. I suggested I went with her and waited in the bar but she said it was too expensive and seemed to prefer that I didn't, so I stayed put. She ran off down the stairs and I watched her in her Lapp-style boots, marching across the snow like a sort of reindeer shepherdess in the dark, towards the bus. Swedes always know when the bus is scheduled to come. It's never late. You run for the bus because it's going to be on time. You time your journey precisely.

Karin and I sat back down where we were and carried on. Swedes aren't a very chatty race of people when you meet them as strangers, on the street - if you try to talk to one they will just as likely cut you dead. But they are different at home, around a kitchen table with a coffee, or *surr* pot on the hob. They'll talk all night, pretty slowly, and may be a bit cumbersome in their style, and not so witty all the time – but they will talk. Karin and I hit it off from the start, and it was pretty kind of her to accept me into her flat, into her kitchen, breaking up the nice twosome they had there, and to make me so welcome. It worked out well, we became a threesome, ate together, sat together, just as she and Lotta had done. I was one of the girls and I always think fondly of that time, and of Karin.

She was perceptive enough to realise that what I was most interested in was Lotta, so she told me a little bit of how they met, which was at school. She said that she was even now quite impressed with herself to be sharing a flat with Lotta as she, Karin, had at first been intimidated by her.

'When we were at school Lotta was one of the tough, bad girls.'

'I find that hard to imagine,' I said. I thought she was joking.

'She was the opposite of what she is now, she was notorious.' I was sure Karin was being sarcastic, or at least exaggerating, but it was an amusing idea anyway. I was quite interested to find out if this was Karin pulling my leg, I had possibly discovered a form of hidden Swedish humour. But she didn't elaborate.

Soon enough it was my time to go and catch the bus. Karin hurried me out into the night, having kitted me out with the right sort of pre-bought tickets, and I caught the bus just in time.

6

otta's directions took me to a part of Stockholm that was more like a conventional European big city. There was much less that was beautiful about it. On the other hand it had buildings that looked as if they had been built by some inspired architects from the 1920s.

I found myself on a raised street that seemed to form a bridge over another street. At each end of the bridge there was a building fifteen stories high, like two sentinel towers, fine and imposing, and a bit like the Nazi style of building, only smaller. At the foot of one of these buildings was a set of stairs that went down to the road below. My directions told me to go down these steps but to turn off half way down and follow a little side street that seemed to hang in mid-air. This was a corner in a big city.

I saw neon signs in English, as if the place was for foreigners, and there was at that time no English anywhere else in Stockholm. There were one or two shops but their front windows had been painted out by psychedelic designs. This was the street I was meant to find, and I started looking for the right number, where I was supposed to wait outside. While I was looking, Lotta suddenly appeared from a small black door more or less right on top of me.

'Oh you're here!' she said and set off with her arm in mine, along the street.

'Where's the bar?' I asked.

'That was it,' she said, and led me to the steps, and we skipped down them and in a flash we were on the busy modern street below.

'I was imagining a bigger, brighter place, for some reason.'

'Oh it is quite big and bright inside.'

'Is that the entrance?'

'Yes it is.'

'Why is it so small?'

'Well, I suppose people go in one at a time,' she said, as if I was merely asking about the size of the door.

'But it had no name on it. How do people know there is a bar here?' I was wondering if that was what bars were like in Sweden, it seemed frustrating and mysterious. 'Aren't people allowed to go to bars in Sweden?' It was an odd question, but what did I know?

'Actually it's not like pubs in England, that's true. You are allowed but you have to queue sometimes.'

'There wasn't a queue for yours.'

She laughed. 'Maybe mine isn't very good or popular,' she suggested. I imagined a sort of cellar with soup-eaters in it. Maybe it was a political bar?

There was a silence. I was already noticing that silences were more normal in Swedish conversations than in English ones, but also that they weren't neutral, they meant all kinds of things, they were used for various purposes. I just didn't know what they were. I tried using one. I waited so long that

I thought the conversation had been dropped. Then;

'I suppose it's more like a sort of club,' she said, by way of a matter-of-fact explanation.

'Oh I see,' I said, trying to picture it. I realised it might be something a bit like the Troubadour, and it all made sense. For a moment I had been trying to picture the pretty sphinx pulling beers in a drinking club for hard-nosed businessmen smoking cigars, wearing suits and discussing Japanese mergers; her mild appearance didn't quite suit.

'Like a folk club?' I asked.

'Yes a bit,' she said. She seemed relieved that I had guessed the sort of thing, and I wondered why she had been embarrassed about it. 'You don't read poetry there do you?' I felt as if I was on the verge of a discovery.

'Oh no, nothing like that. I just work in the bar,' she seemed a bit evasive, so I thought I'd press a bit more to release her from her shyness;

'I'd like to come to the bar next time, especially if it's like a folk club.'

'Oh it's not very much like a folk club, but we do have them I think. Everyone in Sweden knows lots of old songs,' and we went on to talk about old folk songs. I was later to find out that Swedes do indeed know songs and that, at the end of parties, in those days at least, the guitars would come out and songs appear from nowhere.

Soon we were getting on a bus to take us the thirty-five miles north to Lotta's home town. It was exciting. After only a few minutes we left Stockholm and after only a few miles on a big road we were then on a smaller winding road, coated in ice.

I couldn't believe it, the driver didn't slow down at all. Conditions that would have brought any British road to a complete standstill made no impression on Swedish drivers. The bus driver made no concessions at all to the ice, he took the bends and corners without reducing his speed, drove right up to the edge of each bend. Every Swedish road is flanked by a ditch, into which the snow is pushed by ploughs, so one slip and we would have been upside-down. The driver wasn't reckless he was relentless, it wasn't that he drove fast or erratically, it was more that he pressed on at a regular speed that nothing could impede.

I couldn't relax, I watched every inch of road. We sat at the front and I watched the driver too. His movements were almost self-consciously calm and slow, as if the dance he was creating was expressing Sweden's relationship with nature, an imperturbable victory.

The lights of the bus picked out a yellow stream of snow -engulfed country roads, trees, ditches and, every now and then, a red-painted wooden house swerved out of the blackness at us, swooped up to the edge of the road, twirled, weaved and then retreated into the blackness again, as we swished past it. A slow, regular ticking and peeping-noise made the bus sound like a submarine shooting through the depths of a black ocean. The snow was black, only our headlights made it white.

Sometimes the bus stopped to let people out. Sometimes someone got on, showed their monthly pass to the driver as they walked past him, without looking at him. No-one spoke to anyone or even acknowledged their existence, and the only acceptable expression to wear was one of blankness or indifference, and they turned their faces away from one another in a sort of competition over who could seem less to need contact with other people. I looked at them all, no-one looked at me.

The submarine rose slowly to the surface, the road was suddenly lit by big white lights, a petrol station floated by, then another, we were entering a small town. The bus pulled up outside an old train station, where the rails had been long since pulled up. A hamburger kiosk beckoned to me, we got off the bus and I answered the hamburger siren.

We then walked through the town. I could tell that Lotta was proud of this most extraordinary, beautiful wooden town, with low buildings, small shops with one floor above. Up against the walls were the most enormous piles of snow I could ever have imagined.

The snow sloped up sometimes to the upper floor. Gentle lights glowed like candles guttering in saucers of ice. The wooden buildings seemed to grow out of the ice-packed street. The whole thing was like a tunnel. Lotta smiled at me, eyes beaming through her round, steamed-up glasses, pleased with her town, glad that it was behaving itself so well and performing so majestically for me.

We crossed a gaily carved wooden bridge. A few feet below, was a frozen river, where only a trickle of water forced its way down the centre, the rest was frozen. The bridge was at the place where the town met the sea, and looking to my left as we crossed it I saw the flat expanse of grey ice fringed by black forest trees. That was the edge of the Baltic Sea.

After the bridge, there were a few deciduous trees in what

seemed like the remnants of a gay town park that winter had gobbled up and sent to sleep. Then we went up a steep sloping path cut into a rock-like hill, into some woods. Some way up the path there was an ancient looking industrial building, very small.

It was the town's old iron foundry, no bigger than a row of six houses might have been. Icicles the size of pillars hung down from the roof, pointing to the ground they nearly reached. It looked like the cold had stopped the advance of time, those icicles looked like they had been there forever and would forever remain. Steam rose from them or from the building but I didn't know how. Lotta said that the foundry was still working, despite being so old-fashioned. She said a school friend's father had worked there and that the noise from the blast furnace had made him deaf – a side of modern Sweden I didn't really expect.

At the top of the hill, up the road that was really just a track through the woods, we came to a series of wooden villas, charmingly decorated wood-built houses from the turn of the century or before. I marvelled at them, towers and turrets and balconies. We took a turn down a little sloping road at the end of which the frozen sea rose up abruptly; it was another inlet, a small one. You could see across it to the other side four hundred yards away, rocks rising up out of the grey ice and pointed trees making a jagged edge against the moon on top of the rock.

The road was only three houses long, hers was the second, a two-storey iron-oxide red painted wooden house, with white gables and window frames, in the traditional Swedish manner. We walked across the garden buried in snow through which a path had been cut four foot deep.

She pulled out a key from a saucepan on a table under a low-jutting eave by the front door. The door knocker was tiny, a brass fox's head long turned green.

7

Inside it was dark, her parents must be asleep. For some reason I was expecting them to be awake, despite it being late. Didn't they want to see who their daughter brought home?

Inside the house was modern, that is to say 1960s, 70s. Swedish design, very tasteful and pretty, not the glaring miserable white of the modern world, but the grey white of an older Swedish style that had been incorporated into modern design.

A comfortable home with rich walnut and rose wood antiques dotted about, a piano, a red mahogany antique table, a chaise longue in red plush, a real parquet floor you skated on, Swedish rag rugs on the floors, pine table in the kitchen, the kitchen with a classic mustard-yellow set of cupboards in a style from the 1940s with spring latches like you might imagine you'd get on the cupboards in the captain's cabin on a German battleship. It was tidy but not horribly so, quite warm and friendly and confident.

On our way in I had seen that the street ended and the flat white expanse of the sea began, in a bay or inlet from the archipelago. A silent black sky reigned above with princely stars in a flock. Inside the house, the air was motionless in a way air wasn't in any house in Britain; this had the thundering certainty of the juggernaut of electric heat, urging its suit down the pipes and tubes, all in peace and calm. This wasn't Heaven, but it was a very well supported waiting room for Heaven, a clearing house, the best accommodation that perfect good sense could buy.

Lotta took her shoes off and floated in her socks across the parquet floor though the house. I noticed immediately that, while I was a stranger in my parents' new house, she was completely at home here, this was her house. Her childhood was recent enough, I fully expected to see her old toys on the floor. Through the two living-rooms with a piano and sofas we went, though a modern door, still on the ground floor, to an extension, also wooden built, and Lotta's own room.

Another antique bed, this time a single one, white or cream painted with great sweeping curves at each end, in a scroll, like a boat, with lion's feet, and carved along the sides. She saw me staring at it;

'That's my grandmother's bed. It's her wedding present from my grandfather,' she announced.

How odd. Who would give their wife a single bed as a wedding present?

'Don't worry, they had six children. It's where we're going to sleep.' I had hardly time to see the room before we were marched back out to the kitchen to eat the routine sandwiches of cheese and caviar. We kissed standing against the fridge. I was troubled by her parents being upstairs, Lotta wasn't. Although she had a way of limiting mouth contact at times, as if she felt it too intimate, while her body in a subtle unmoving way, went in the opposite direction, and seemed already to be making its way back to the strange single bed.

Back in the bedroom, Lotta adorned herself in a long plain nightdress, like a cotton tube, the most unattractive garment I could have imagined for her – and got into the bed. I wore my clothes, a peculiarity of mine. That bed was the narrowest I have ever seen, we had to cling onto each other just to avoid falling out.

Movement wasn't really possible. She lay facing me, her beautiful face inches from me, a wide friendly smile, a smell as fresh as the air in a forest emanated from her, my heart jumped and started racing. I could feel her naked body against the soft cotton of her tube, the rolling forms of her voluptuousness captured within her slight frame and concealed as ever. The transcendent beauty of her face paralysed my mind, anaesthetised it, prior to it being devoured by the mythic beast of the forest.

If it hadn't been for an eventuality, the next bit *would* be about my further discovery of her legs which God had ordained should be the best legs on his favourite planet and about what it felt like to find myself on intimate terms with the charismatic holders of such a title, to find them showing willingness towards me as if they had just been any old attractive legs, about how they had the same enigmatic quality of, say, a famous mathematician or painter or poet, or as if you would see Newton or Byron or Rembrandt in real life and see that they were, despite their greatness, contained nevertheless within the compass of five feet and some inches of the frail human frame, that their existence in actual fact extended no further than the limits of their own physical bounds, whereas the charisma of their essence extended far beyond that; yes this page would have been about the paradox of the charm of beauty of the first rank that I had only just begun to get to see or feel, had not some badgers chosen to have the most ferocious of fights under the house, directly beneath our bed. I had never heard such a sound and I didn"t know anything about badgers, or the way they fought. I had never seen one.

It sounded like one had sunk its teeth into the other and refused to let go; a fierce mortal combat, a screaming and tearing, thrashing, crashing and banging that wouldn't stop, a few feet beneath us in the empty space beneath the floorboards. Lotta said her father was always having the badgers shot but they keep coming back 'they must like living here.' I pointed out that it couldn't be the same ones unless they were immortal. Morning came before we fell asleep, those legs wrapped around me somehow.

I found breakfast a bit embarrassing.

I just couldn't get used to the idea that someone, anyone, was allowed to sleep in their daughter's bed without her parents taking the opportunity to meet them first, since we were all in the house anyway. I think I was a prude. She was allowed to take anyone she liked into her bedroom, into that tiny little bed.

A black thought of her taking others there crossed my mind, stamping on the fairy tale palace of her eyes, but the thought was extinguished as incompatible with her. These examples of middle-class modern liberal virtue, her parents, greeting me with their open, friendly and civilized grace, didn't quite fool me though; their coldness made me feel like a dirty little Irish urchin who had unspeakably, unthinkably besmirched their beautiful daughter, a fact which they were dealing with in a friendly, smiling way.

Despite their easy manner, conversation was a little stilted across the bread and coffee table. I was desperate for tea but there was none; 'They only give me tea when I'm ill,' Lotta explained. I was fingers and thumbs as I tried to negotiate the strictly relaxed manners of the Swedish table. There was a lot of passing things around and around and yet I got the feeling I was eating too much and passing around too little.

Lotta's mother spoke in riddles, long, slow, indirect sentences in very good English, mainly about arrangements, buses and what was going to be eaten at the next meal (after it had been passed round a few times). Her father spoke eloquently and like a BBC presenter. I felt as if my own English was not really fit for the breakfast table. Lotta was at ease and quite jolly, if a little like an unfriendly teenager towards her parents. I felt I wanted to demonstrate my goodwill towards them to compensate, but it wasn't my good will they wanted, it was hers, and they weren't very receptive to me. I had the feeling I was too loud and my sentences were too long, so I tried to shorten them. I made a mental note to keep my answers short, but I was to find that brevity of that calibre was not within a normal person's capacity.

After breakfast, Lotta's father asked me about my trousers.

He asked if I wanted to borrow a pair of his. My own, he pointed out, had paint stains on them.

I looked down. True enough, there were some flecks of paint, a few different colours, of oil paint from when I had been painting that silly self-portrait back in London. I didn't know quite what to say.

I declined his offer of the trousers, although I'm not altogether sure he meant it seriously since he was easily four inches taller than me. I didn't fancy wearing his trousers anyway, though of course I didn't say so. I was aware that saying no to his trousers left the situation the same; paint stains on my trousers which were bothersome to him. I had never encountered this kind of thing before, except from my own mother. Other people's mothers and fathers tended to take me as they found me and mind their own business. I was in a corner and there was no obvious way out. I didn't have the money for new trousers and I didn't like the idea of having to buy new clothes to suit her parents anyway. I was learning the rule; relaxed casual-wear was compulsory – and it must be clean.

He asked too, in a more or less friendly way, if there was any reason why I dressed the way I did. What was the thinking behind it, he wondered. Now, I tended to wear black trousers, a white shirt, a black waistcoat and a black or grey suit jacket. He asked if it was a parody of his generation. I said it wasn't. He asked if I had anything against jeans and a t-shirt; they would be happy to pay for me to buy some, Lotta and I could go down to town in the afternoon.

This was quite beyond what I could have expected from anyone. The rules of liberal, modern Sweden were strictly enforced on all levels it seemed, at least in this middle class household. I told him I had never worn jeans, which was a lie, and squeezed out of the room.

I told Lotta about it. 'They can't understand what you look like,' she said, with a funny look on her face, but otherwise no vocal outburst of defiance. I began to wonder where I had landed.

She suggested we go on a trip to Finland, and it seemed like a very good idea to me. She already knew the boat times and we just had enough time to catch the next one, if her father drove us to the port which was twenty miles away, which he was glad to do. He seemed to enjoy introducing me to the scenery along the way with a magnanimous sweep of the arm indicating the pine trees, lakes and such like. Sweden has eighteen billion pine trees, apparently.

The port of Kappelskär was pretty simple, but the ships were very big; giant ferries to go the twelve-hour trip across the Baltic to Finland. It was tremendously exciting to find myself in these places, a world I had no previous knowledge of, or thoughts of. I only just about knew where these countries were.

The stillness snow imparts gave the impression of permanence to the piles of freight waiting to travel. The sparseness and logicality of the accommodation for passengers was still unfamiliar to me, this world of quiet efficiency in the face of the grinding presence of the snow. Still less had I anticipated the sea. It wasn't sea, it was ice. The ships sailed through a corridor, a narrow path had been cut through it by the icebreakers.

The path was no wider than the ship itself, and to me it seemed as if the ferry was cutting its *own* way though the ice. The silence that the ice created was broken only by the deep rumble of the engine and the scrape and bump of the lumps of ice that bobbed and thrust themselves up to the bulwarks of the ship. It was an incredible sight to me, I had always thought ships sank if they went anywhere near ice. The glistening perfection of ice-floes covered the hidden dark of the water beneath.

We sailed past hundreds of tiny islands in the archipelago, so close that you could see the birds shivering on the trees.

There were many Finns on the ship of course. They seemed harder and rougher that the Swedes, an impression which grew as the hours passed and they had spent more time in the bars. I was used to Irish drinking, this was similar but of a different kind. More resolute even, more joyless. This was the drinking of a people who otherwise seemed to say very little, dour and self-contained. At around two in the morning I saw a man in a suit pissing onto the carpet in the corridor; he seemed to actually believe he was in the urinal, so drunk was he.

There were gypsies on the ship too, real Romanys, black haired, sallow-skinned, dark-eyed people. The men wore trousers like jodhpurs with knee-high boots of black leather. The women wore huge crinolines, with bustles and fine white lace and head-dresses. They all took an interest in me. I could feel them looking at me, wondering. Eventually they beckoned me over. They liked the rings on my fingers and of course my jet black hair, blacker than theirs.

They asked if I was a gypsy. I explained that I wasn't a gypsy, but that I was Irish. They were the friendliest people I had met so far in Scandinavia except the ones I had got to know, like Erkki, and Karin. These gypsies didn't seem to have anything to do with anyone else, kept themselves to themselves. They gave us coffee and cakes, but we didn't share a language. I felt though, for a few moments, as if I belonged somewhere. It was a nice illusion. They invited us to visit them in Finland, which we did, some weeks later.

Eventually the ship subsided into drink-induced sleep. Lotta and I lay down on the floor behind some chairs.

She did the strangest thing as we lay there; she put her bag with her clothes in it between us, like Tristan's sword to protect her chastity. It was bizarre, I felt offended. Did she think I couldn't keep my hands off her even though we were in public? Where did she get that idea, that habit of thought? I lay there in the half-light thinking about it. I didn't feel very happy.

It was after only a few hours of sleep on the floor that the ship docked in Helsinki. I struggled to my feet and off we went.

I remember sitting in the harbour tram that was to take us into town, staring at the tramtracks and thinking about that business with the bag between us. One angry part of me felt like going home, was telling me that this girl was trouble. It was inexplicable to me.

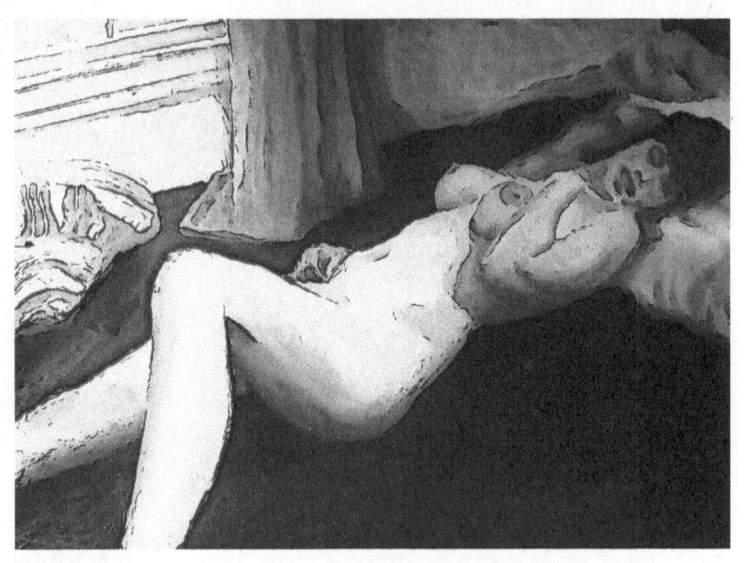

8

Helsinki was a far more dour and forbidding city than Stockholm. It looked as if Soviet Russian architects had built parts of it, great grey-brown phalanxes and wide streets. The snow looked even colder than it did in Sweden, and life seemed harder. I felt as if I had gone very far east. I was Fitzroy Maclean and Elroy Flecker and I had boldly taken the golden road to Samarkand.

We went looking for somewhere to stay immediately. It was daunting to be just out on the streets as the temperature was minus thirty-two degrees and my clothes were inadequate.

Within minutes, Lotta had found a sort of 'pension,' a Nordic bed and breakfast without the breakfast. A shuffling man shuffled us along a dark, wall-papered corridor behind a bar or café, to a room on the ground floor. A door like those you have in Paris apartments, a double wooden door, thick and heavy, and there we were in the most extraordinary room I had ever seen. The floorboards were deep reddish brown, as was all the woodwork, the walls were papered with a faded pattern from seventy years ago and in the corner was a round or rather, cylinder-shaped tiled-stove reaching right the way up to the high ceiling, the kind of thing I had only seen at the National Theatre in sets for Chekhov plays. It had tiny brass doors and a small place for burning wood, but could keep the minus thirty degrees cold out for hours due to a complicated system of tiny passages where the smoke and hot air circulated.

The only furniture was a bed which was most oddly placed in the centre of the room, not against a wall, like where you'd normally put a table. It was a single bed of ancient construction, not unlike Lotta's own bed.

We went straight for it and slept a very mysterious sleep of absolute exhaustion. I was sharply aware of having travelled way beyond anything I could call familiar or recognizable. I was in the Wild West except it was the East, and the prairies were snow-covered and hostile. Distances and temperatures swirled about in my brain while I slept, voices came along the corridor. Lotta had been resolute about sleeping and, as we went to sleep, she said something about having an appointment at five o'clock.

That piece of information joined the voices coming and going in the corridor and danced about in my sleeping mind, a curious, ill-favoured dance.

I woke up, she was gone. A note read;

You were so deep asleep that I didn't wake you, but I had to go to meet those boring weaving girls I told you about from my school in Åland. I won't be long, very boring, I come back here at nine. I am at Kapteeninkatu 11, it's not very far from here but don't bother coming there, it will be so great when I get back we will look around Helsinki together love and kisses. Lotta

A nice kettle of fish.

Oh well. Hm, she hadn't actually told me about those friends, unless of course I had fallen asleep while she was telling me. I wished she had woken me though. Never mind, not to worry, I had time to kill now. A walking tour around Helsinki? Maybe just a cup of coffee. Strange to be in that alien city and the reason for being there, gone to a weavers' party. I knew Lotta had done weaving, I had seen the results. A very pale blue rag rug. No, I would find out what an evening alone in Helsinki would be like, it's a good time of day anyway. What part of town was I in? Kapteeninkatu sounded like it had to do with captains, ships' captains, we might be near the harbour. Who knows? The room I was in was probably near the docks too.

I wandered down the corridor to where the smell of coffee came from, and found a small dark cafe with a few old men in it. I went in and ordered a coffee from whom I recognied as our host. He was neither Swedish nor wholly Finnish I thought. He had a very broad face and was blonde gone slate-grey. I later learned that this was indeed a Finnish look, they were Huns. His face was about one hundred years old while his body was about forty. He smoked continuously. He knew I was staying in his room, I think the building was full of such rooms. I just couldn't work out who would be staying in them. It didn't seem to be for foreign tourists certainly, nor for families, maybe it was for workmen. It seemed very old, as if nothing had changed there for fifty years. Small, dark, brown and wooden, full of smoke and time and smells. It was the kind of place that was alive and that you just can't find now anywhere, no matter where you go. I didn't realise at the time that I was on the edge of history, looking back. I smoked a few cigarettes there with my coffee and I was beginning to enjoy myself, the feeling of being in a small, brown alien world that was moving slowly around me, like a bull around a matador. No-one looked at anyone still, there in that cafe, just like in Sweden, everyone sat alone.

One thing you could clearly have for yourself in Scandinavia was space and anonymity; people left you alone. You could be on your own and stay alone, no-one was going to trouble you, or even see you. That's what I thought and I was beginning to enjoy it.

'*Mustalainen!*' Suddenly a big blond Finn was standing behind my chair. I had no idea where he had come from. Not from the door to the cafe, it was closed. This guy was pretty drunk and he was ready to fight.

'*Mustalainen!!!*' *(*Finnish for 'gypsy') he yelled at me. I didn't know what it meant but it wasn't an invitation to a game of cards. He took a swipe at me and I ducked. I was up out of my chair in a shot and put the table between him and me. He advanced through the table as if it wasn't there.

'He thinks you're a gypsy,' said one of the old men in there, who suddenly seemed to know I was English-speaking, or I guess at least foreign. 'You'd better leave.'

This piece of advice, given free and with no other content, such as solidarity of sympathy, rubbed me up the wrong way. I'm not especially brave when I know I am going to get my head knocked off for sure, but I'm bad-tempered enough if provoked, to be a bit of an optimist, and this feller, though big and wild, a killer, was just about too drunk to catch me, and I knew it.

I explained to him in North London English, that he was a cunt and that I was indeed a gypsy, and I was going to cut his throat with my knife made of diamonds and donkey bone, and I invited him to fuck himself. Then I stepped back and to the side, just in time for him to slam his fist into the wall.

You could hear his knuckles crack. He wasn't so drunk that it didn't hurt, and I left him to contemplate. I took the advice of my cold comfort friend and left, and wished them all a good evening.

Notwithstanding my lucky escape, I was feeling pretty down after that and a bit shaken. How many more Finns regarded me in the same way? Gone were the anonymity and isolation. Suddenly I was walking through the crowd with a neon sign above my head, pointing down at me.

`I spent the next hour racked by the usual angry vengeful fantasies that accompany fright and humiliation at the hands of another man, followed by the usual forgiveness and warmth, a pretty humiliating charade in itself. I reverted to anger and tried to find a position where I didn't care too much, and tried to return to my serenity and detachment.

By this time I had walked into an area that was empty, big and ugly enough to be the docks. I asked for Kapteeninkatu but was told it was three kilometres away along a road that turned out to be a featureless trail along a perimeter fence. I almost gave up, but the idea of Lotta walking there by herself worried me a bit.

I was enjoying Helsinki even though it was big and cold and hostile. It was so cold my nostrils stuck together when I breathed, and I was still horribly under-dressed, despite having a few layers of vests, some long johns and so on, under my clothes.

Luckily, dry cold doesn't penetrate as much as the damp cold of Britain, so minus thirty degrees can be strangely bearable. But I was walking too far and eating too little. I was beginning to feel weak and my hands were shaking. The empty road with its fence stretched out before me, I needed to get back to civilisation.

There was almost no-one around but when anyone came past I asked for Kapteeninkatu and it never got any closer. At last there was a kiosk where you could get food and I picked up something called a *pirog* which was the most welcome food I had eaten since the milk of childhood. I never would have chosen pie pastry filled with rice and grey meat but there it was, tasting like manna maybe tasted. It was the best food I'd had since arriving in the North and I went back and bought another two to keep me going. The wind was now blowing in from somewhere, and I couldn't think straight enough to work out where it might be coming from.

At last I got off that long road, and found Kapteeninkatu. It seemed like I had walked in a big circle, and at last I was on proper streets with a few shops and cafes. I passed a small cinema and some clubs of some kind. It was early evening and people were beginning to come out and look as if they wanted entertainment. The buildings had the usual four of five storeys above street level. The building corresponding to the street address I had was an unremarkable, rather drab, brown building from around 1920, not very attractive, unadorned and dreary, but at least unspoiled by renovation or anything of that kind.

It had only one shop on the ground floor and that was a kind of sound equipment shop, with a load of loudspeakers of the older kind, huge black monsters, piled up in the windows. It was more of a repair shop than a shop. A few motorbikes stood outside, some British bikes amongst them, BSA, Triumph; their owners must have been milling about inside. There were also some American cars there, in pretty rough condition but running. I had already noticed that was a bit of a thing in Sweden and Finland, young men, what we might call greasers, driving around in American cars.

I pushed open the door to the building, and went inside to the lobby. The door crashed shut behind me with an almighty clatter that went right up the stairwell.

The address was for the first floor, so I walked up. I wanted only to look at the door and go away again, downstairs to wait, for no particular reason other than having nothing more interesting to do.

There were three apartments on that floor, all unmarked except by name, there were no numbers. I stood and listened outside each door and they were all silent.I peeped through the letterboxes of each, and saw more or less the same thing, coats hanging up, boots in the rack, and no sign of anyone, except the smell of cooking.

I listened for voices, just out of curiosity, but there weren't any. I went back down the stairs filled with the presence of those domestic households, the smells of their dinners they had eaten, each family had its own smells of course, I was pleased to have experienced three from this far off land.

On the ground floor I saw a door I hadn't noticed on my way up; it led out to the courtyard at the back. On the door was written; '*Holgersson Film*'. Those words could have been Swedish or English, but not Finnish. Nothing more. It seemed interesting but it wasn't what I was looking for, so I went back out into the street, asked someone the time. It was already past nine o'clock in the evening.

Lotta had been away five hours now, so I guessed she might likely be about to leave, or had already left. I thought I'd head back to the room. A small stream of people came out of the door to the building, they looked a bit like roadies or something, so I presumed they were to do with the words on the door. They got on the motorbikes and into the American cars. After a few moments of the roaring of engines, they sped off.

Still no sign of any weaving girls. I was enjoying getting my view of Helsinki, in my own way while Lotta was with her old folkcraft classmates. There was no real reason why she should be there, they had probably gone to a cafe anyway, and she had gone straight home.

Within forty-five minutes, after getting lost only once, I was back at the strange room. I had left the door open for Lotta to get back in, we had no luggage anyway, and nothing to steal.

Lotta was already there, fast asleep in the tiny old bed. She was wrapped up and curled up, only the brown gold of her hair was visible, tangled and stretched out across the white pillowcase. I moved quietly so as not to wake her and was wondering if I should go out for a beer or something to let her sleep - when she woke up.

She said she had only been there for fifteen minutes, 'Just having a short sleep,' she said. She looked as if she had been asleep for eight hours. She confessed to being exhausted.

'Shall we go out?' I suggested. It was only ten o'clock and, unlike in England, the bars were still open for hours yet.

'No, I can't I'm too tired. Those girls are so boring, they tire me out. I get so sleepy when I see them, I can't move. Don't you want to sleep too?'

I wasn't sure if she meant I should really go to sleep. Even though we had only just met, she knew I never slept before three in the morning. 'I could read next to you in bed, ' I said, 'if you're too tired to get up.'

So I did. She turned and faced me and her whole body was flowing like ice out of a volcano. The bed was literally hot, and she rolled and flowed so that I was burned like a shrub in the path of orange fire from the centre of the earth.

Her molten body was once more contained within her drab nightdress cotton tube, which somehow rolled up to become a short skirt that I didn't even dare look at for more than a second, stretched high up across those thighs of hers. I had to keep my head, I had to literally hold her off or I wouldn't have lasted more than one minute. She wanted everything all at once, and she glowed like coal and pulsated inside and out, her eyes were so alive they were weak and swimming, as if she had a fever, maybe she did, she was very warm. My heart was racing, I was on a runaway carriage and I had to hold on or be swept away. I was burned out by that burning mountain a few times that night and taken down to into the hell-fire depths of the earth, for that is all hell-fire is, at its very worst and its very best. You could take me there any time, I saw ahead of me a life of riding to hell on the back of this lamb, or pony, or demon, whatever she was, one thousand miles to the centre of the earth. You could leave me there in the ashes at the end of it, and put it on my tombstone that I died the day the world screamed. I knew I'd never forget that room, I was impressed the bed an floorboards didn't catch fire or the window melt back into sand. One thing was for sure, there was something so wrong with that girl that it was right, so right that nothing could stand up next to it, and whatever it was, the world could only ever say yes to it.

Finally she fell asleep, her tiredness had never left her, she was carving rocks out of tiredness throughout it all, and as I lay there like a broken wheel, I mused upon a few things, about what made her like that, and why she unleashed it in that place, on that evening, and I wondered why, despite all the wildness inside her, she never for one second looked anything less than a perfect statue, a painted beauty shining through the flesh that was no flesh, flames that were cool, white and round like marble; if a nordic god would have a whore or a lover it would be her. Asleep beside me, her face mild and beatific, she looked once again like one of God's angels.

We sizzled our way back across the ice of the Baltic in the giant ferry, the next day. The ice helped to cool her off, like a red-hot iron in a pail of water. She had to be back at school the following day. We spent one more night in her parents' house and I lay next to her, terrified she would again ignite, only yards from her parents' room upstairs. I felt sure that proximity wouldn't bother her, but she made do with the coasting speed of a racing car pulling into a pit stop and by God that was enough for any man. She was only dormant. In this way she was the easiest person in the world to satisfy. She reminded me, in my limited experience of life, of one of those things they used to have at my school fete, when you had to move a ring around a curved electric bar, and if your hand shook it buzzed and you had to start again. The least movement set it off and released the electricity.

The following morning, another breakfast. Her parents stayed behind their newspapers.

Back in Stockholm, Lotta had only one week left of school before the holiday, and we got into a routine for that week. She went off to school and I stayed at home, worked on a painting of her room and one of her kitchen, drank weak beer (1.2%) and smoked cigarettes, then went to meet her for lunch in the taxi-rank cafe.

'Is the Englishman going to have soup today?' asked the round lady, each day, in exactly the same tone and rhythm of voice, and I always had the pea and ham soup, with those same three rolls, ham, liver pate, and cheese, a glass of milk and a coffee.

In the evening we listened to music on her tiny record player; she had three records; Jimi Hendrix, Bob Dylan and Duke Ellington, and that's all anyone seemed to need.

We broke her bed. I mention it only because it's one of the things that happened, but it had nothing to do with sexual vigour; there was never anything energetic or acrobatic or gymnastic about us when we had sex.

The bed broke from her psychic energy. It broke, there was no reason for it to break, except that she was having an orgasm and the bed suddenly lurched to the side and the mattress dropped about twelve inches. Nothing we did, or nothing I did certainly, caused it. It was like Jung's exploding bookcase. That had frightened Freud, who witnessed it (in fact it was *his* bookcase and Jung exploded it) and Lotta's exploding bed put the wind up me a bit too. It took me a whole day to mend it. I hadn't really learnt carpentry yet then. I didn't want the tall aristocratic man to hate me more than he already did. I could easily imagine him going up there to inspect Lotta's bed when we were out.

Lotta's plan for the next weekend, still the one preceding when I was supposed to arrive, was to go and visit her grandfather. I met the idea with a bit of caution, having already tasted life with his son, Lotta's father. Apparently this grandfather was a powerful oil magnate, a domineering bully of a man who had built up Sweden's only oil company and its only oil refinery.

He owned ships and sent them all around the world to collect oil. The oil company was remarkable for being a co-operative and a consequence of this was that, while he was rich, he wasn't super rich. Such was this man's personality that Lotta's father was intimidated by him, throughout his whole life. I couldn't wait to meet him. And I felt sure that he would love me as a son the moment he set eyes on me.

Lotta didn't seem to be at all worried about my reception. We duly set off from the Central Station, to the south of Sweden, to Helsingborg, near where the oil magnate lived. Lotta said we could combine the trip with a visit to Copenhagen.

After the train and a bus we rolled up looking like ideal company for the master of Swedish oil; me in my London Oxfam 'parody' clothes with paint stains, and Lotta, a not very glamorously presented vegetarian, a bluebird startled in the bullrushes, on the outside, and a sleeping devil on the inside

The moment I met the grandfather I knew he didn't like Lotta's homespun persona. In fact, I knew it when I saw his wife, who was a handsome, very expensive-looking woman whose features had clearly done more than their fair share in creating the beauty in clogs and corduroys by my side.

The oil magnate stood on the doorstep of his three-wing house twenty yards from the sea, we stood below him on the gravel. He had pretty good businessman's English in which he welcomed me. He was a relatively short man with a powerful face and eyebrows. He had an ingrained mischievous look on him, a sort of fiendish cunning mixed with a fair degree of intelligence.

But I knew he was a drinker. And I knew he was drunk. And I therefore knew that he was retired from business life and that his hands were now off the reins of business, and that his keen interest in the two dishevelled creatures before him showed he had time on his hands to cause trouble. I saw at once that the fingers of his left hand were twitching. These fingers were the vehicle of his pent-up energy and frustration, and they worked constantly, grinding and twitching, twinkling like nasty stubby stars. This was going to be fun.

His wife, slightly more cunning than even he, but lazier, made a languid effort to welcome us both in a friendly way. I was forewarned however, that this was the grandmother who used to give Lotta fiercely short haircuts when she was a child, presumably to make her less pretty.

We were shown to our wing of the house, not as grand as it sounds but grand enough, and told that dinner was served in twenty-five minutes.

We assembled in the main house. There was a whole rigma-role of standing behind your chair before sitting down; one of the many rigmaroles the famously relaxed Swedes impose upon their young foreign guests. I felt like Gawain on his way to find the Green Knight, enjoying all the various forms of malevolent hospitality that stood between him and his voluntary execu-tion. *Gawain and the Green Knight* was actually in my bag, I wondered should I go and fetch it to show it to my host.

He was pretty well oiled by now and the main event was the bitter jibes directed at him by his handsome wife, and the jolly way he parried them by flirting with his beautiful grand-daugh-ter. He seemed to like me a bit, in that he could tell I was a good audience for his antics, his persona and his boasting. I was especially interested to hear about his safaris in the 1960s with his wife and their friends, which Lotta had asked about. Lotta took out from the shelf a photo album devoted to it, and it looked like stills from a Hollywood movie of the 1950s.

My joy was crowned when I learned that Lotta's parents were coming down to join the party the next evening. Lotta had forgotten this clash but said that it would be all right as they would have the rooms above us and we wouldn't really see them much.

After dinner, Lotta took me on a secret tour of the house. It was a bit scary. We could see her grandfather smoking out in the garden, and as long as we could see him the coast was clear.

She had the nerve to take me into the old man's personal little room, whence he had been banished by his wife twenty years previously for his infidelities and his drinking. It was a tiny little room, an old man's room. I remembered hearing that the Queen of England was rumoured to have a little room like this somewhere inside Buckingham Palace, where she actually lived, made her baked beans on toast and watched TV. Lotta told me the oil magnate had a revolver in the drawer and to my horror she whipped open a drawer beside the bed and there it lay.

'I'm not allowed in here,' she said. 'Once, when I was little, my grandmother caught me in here and she actually hit me.' Unheard of in Sweden.

I was glad to get out of there. From the house you could more or less see Hamlet's castle, Elsinore, which they call Kronborg, and it was there we set off to the next day.

Lotta was quite keen to get an early train and I didn't mind despite losing sleep as it meant not meeting her grandparents. We got up so early in fact that she gave me a guided tour of the tiny seaside town where her grandparents lived, where one house after another was one where she had played as a child.

She had obviously spent a lot of time there. It was a picturesque little harbour with pleasure yachts and boats for the well-off. The Skaggerak Sea lowered out in the mist and all the previous night we had listened to the mist sirens, a series of foghorns whose mournful cries kept the boats from running aground.

It was a beautiful enough place with a saga-like atmosphere due to the proximity of another country, so close you could see the traffic.

This part of Sweden had once belonged to Denmark and the cruel and bloody hand of the lunatic Kristian II had held it in its iron grip.

Denmark was still an exotic idea to the Swedes, wilder and rougher, belonging somehow to the continental south. Copenhagen especially was somewhere they loved to go, a cosmopolitan city with a less controlled toughness than Stockholm. It was where Sweden went to drink and behave badly. They had drugs and prostitutes and Hell's Angels and lawlessness in Christiania, an impossibility in conformist Sweden. I had glimpsed Copenhagen on my way to Sweden, now I was going to see it through different eyes.

Lotta took me to see the little mermaid, a statue of a Hans Christian-Andersen character, who sits forever with her siren song sadly in the sea, at the edge of Copenhagen. Then we went to a place called *Huset* literally the building, or the house, a giant pub for Scandinavian hippies, a huge, wooden, four-storied series of bars that had stopped wonderfully in the late 1960s.

Beer slopped around the floor and flowed down the wooden stairs. Big Danes with golden hair, wooden clogs and wild clothes sat drinking huge tankards of beer.

It was nothing like an English pub. It was like being on the pages of *Asterix the Gaul* where warriors quaffed the magic potion to help them in their fight against civilisation. I was enjoying the time machine aspect of it. It's always a relief to be liberated from the confines of the present handed out to us. It was impossible to imagine these people went home at night, or what kind of lives they led. They looked as if they were always there, always drinking, always drunk, always in Huset, always in those clothes, always young, always strong, always living to excess, never suffering the consequence, never declining.

I was so intoxicated with it that I thought Lotta had already spent her youth there in that place, that she was a time-traveller from the 1960s too, that she had been drinking and smoking for an eternal youth. In reality she and I wrestled with the two small beers and smoked not nearly enough cigarettes, although I'd never seen her smoke at all before, she smoked now and looked like a child smoking and I told her so.

She laughed and said she had been exactly that, and that 'when I was fourteen I was smoking twenty-five per day or more, I smoked as soon as I woke up.' I was shocked. She looked about fourteen now, God knows what she must have looked like when she was actually fourteen. I felt moved as I watched her sitting there doodling aimlessly on the back of a cigarette packet. She looked momentarily very small and lost.

Once again, she announced she had some friends to meet, and once again she was afraid I wouldn't like them;

'They were my friends when I was here in the summers, and they are just boring Swedes that study here and they are just like my grandparents only in miniature, you wouldn't like that would you? If I see them now I won't have to go and visit them one by one in Stockholm this summer when they go there.'

'Should I wait here?'

'Yes, wait here. You can write poems here and no-one will bother you; they don't mind blackheads in Denmark,' she joked. She joked but she looked bothered about the afternoon, as I was. I had a fear of not being able to find her again. Copenhagen seemed even bigger than Helsinki, though not as cold and forbidding.

'So,' she stood up with her bag in her hand, 'I go to see the boring girls now.' We arranged that she would be back in five-hours time, just like in Helsinki. 'They go to bed early these weaving girls,' I ventured.

She looked uneasy.

'You don't have to go if you don't want to. Why not wait and see them in the summer?' She looked like she wanted to do as I said.

'I can't, I've promised now, I'd better get it over and done with. It will be nice afterwards, you'll see.'

For some reason my heart sank as I watched her go. It didn't feel right, it didn't make as much sense as it was supposed to. I felt as if we were inviting bad luck, the mist sirens were still in my head with their sorry lament. What if I could never find her again? Suddenly the world seemed like a very big place, and she so small within it. I could still see her slight form as she picked her way through the Viking hoards on the beer-sodden benches. She looked like a butterfly collector, in a meadow with bulls in it, with an unrealistic net full of holes.

I nearly got up to go after her, but some terrible sense of purpose in her movements held me back when it should have driven me forwards.

She was gone.

And the longest five hours of my life so far, began. I realised that she had given me no address, unlike last time. She was cut loose and adrift. We had no means of contact, I had no actual way of finding her again.

Why did it bother me so much more this time? What was the feeling I had about it? It was surely the most natural thing in the world for her to go somewhere. We weren't joined at birth, why should I be in contact with her now, this afternoon? We had been oblivious to each other for nineteen years and survived and found each other, we would surely find each other again, in a few hours as arranged. All I had to do was to sit right there where I was and not move. All she had to do was to come back. Stay alive and come back.

The hairs on my neck stood up. What in the name of God was that stray thought? Why did it press into my head? I feared my own intuition even though I knew it might be mistaken and could lead me astray. Stay alive. All she had to do was stay alive and come back.

Suddenly everything seemed to be like a dream. Ghosts were walking around in my mind and taking up words and gestures and throwing them in my face, right up close and amplified, like warnings and signs. I had to stand up. I flew down the three flights of stairs and out onto the street. I hoped to God that I would be able to catch sight of her. I looked until it hurt, I looked until all my equilibrium was gone; I looked until the dogs of panic and havoc had been set loose inside my mind, and I knew they would not rest until this was over one way or another.

There was no sight of her. I knew, and I don't know how I knew, that she had gone in a taxi. There were no taxis around but in my minds eye I saw her getting into one, and the vision of it scared me. It told me something. It told me she wasn't going to see any boring girls, it told me she had something else to do and I had no earthly idea what it was.

My only comfort was that I realised I didn't know her.

Or… that I might not know her. The illusion was that I did indeed know her. Without really speaking or without there being anything to report, we had seemed to find each other. I think I presumed she was going to be my wife, and I think she thought so too.

But at the same time we were strangers, strangers born for one another, but unknown to one another. And in that I took a cold refuge, I thought, 'Well, if I don't know her then I am nowhere near her, and therefore I cannot lose her as I don't have her; she is an illusion, a stranger.'

But this comfort was swept away with each moment I recalled the connection when we were together, a simple and unelaborate, non-worldly complexity, just a very simple marriage, already made, as they say, in the stars. That was enough to throw me back into the jaws of panic. Where in God's name was she?

I drifted in and out of the two ideas as I stood there on the street as good as blind. I couldn't see two feet in front of me, though my eyes tried to take it all in, I couldn't. A grey sheet of fear fell down, wiped away all the blue and yellow and red. I searched where I could, my eyes were useless, I searched for sounds, there was only a hum, I searched my memory but it was only filled with ghosts. Ghosts of her, trailing clues.

The cigarette packet! I tuned and ran back up the three flights of stairs, back to our table. It was gone. The cigarette packet was gone. The table was cleared away and empty. I looked around wildly, my eyes were swimming. A waitress was emptying a tray into the bin, and I fished out the contents, including the cigarette packet.

And there it was. The note. The note I knew she had written on the cigarette box.

'If you can't find me, I am at - ' and the address. It was like emerging from under water after nearly drowning. I could breathe again.

I sat cradling the box at first, doing nothing, trying to gather my thoughts and put myself back together again so I could think clearly.

To calm down, think slower, take more into consideration and quell the panic. To maybe even realise that nothing was amiss, that now I had more control I could keep disaster at bay by doing almost nothing.

There was no longer any need to run, I could walk. All I had to do at most, was to go there, to that address, wherever it was, and wait.

I'd probably, despite everything, find her yawning with some boring girls, eating a pile of cakes. I could even sit down and wait here if I wanted to. I could wait and see what the passing of hours would tell me, if it brings me anywhere nearer the truth.

That's what I did. I sat back down at a beer-drenched table. I bought a coffee, but before it arrived I recalled the sight of Lotta writing the message, and I asked myself; Why didn't she tell me she was writing the address there? Quite simply, she must have been in two minds about whether to give it to me, that's why she left it to chance. Why was she in two minds? What were these two minds saying? She looked so small and frail writing that message, I remembered the moment. And then, minutes later, so purposeful, picking her way through the tables away from me.

Thirty five years later, Lotta and I were walking along the parapet of Hamlet's castle one evening on our way back from Sweden, we had just read the manuscript of this book together, the one you have in your hands. It hadn't taken long, it's a short book, short because I wanted to stop before our lives together really began.

We were both moved to see ourselves so young, and by the sense of longing we got simply from seeing things described, objects, people, times gone by. We were also moved to see the beginnings of our love, picturesque and romantic but only a candle compared to the fire of our love for one another now.

Lotta said, 'You know what's missing though?'

I said, 'The secret of what you were up to?'

She said, 'God no! Don't tell that! No, I mean the poem you wrote while you waited for me at the table in Huset'

I said, 'I didn't write a poem then. That's funny, how you've got it muddled up! You mean of course the song I wrote there, sitting in the same place, ten years later,'.

'Yes, that's the one. Of course. I mean, is it right to tell only the easy part of such an important thing as life-long love?'

'Hm, maybe not.'

'It could be accused of being misleading.'

'Well I have put in a few hints of a darker side.'

'Only the beginning of it.'

'Well....'

'Of course I wish I *had* been only mischievous, as you suggest, but that's not really the whole story is it?

The song she meant was one I wrote when I was changing trains in Copenhagen on my way to Stockholm, much like the journey described in this book, but in quite different circumstances - in the middle of a storm, so to speak.

Lotta looked out over the castle walls and across the Sound to Sweden, and she started to whistle the tune.

The words to the song were these:

This is the night train to the north to fetch my baby home.
I've never in my life felt so afraid and so alone.
A thousand Belgian cattle lying dead on the grass,
As the guard comes past wearing his death mask.
The evening light hides my tears,
As we crawl into the dark and disappear

'Why did you ever let her go away?'
Ask the bells of La Chapelle as they pass away.
I can't bear to look at the Black Beast Of Cologne,
Because it seems to ask me why I let her go away alone.
They'll have to bury my soul in a box in Düsseldorf
If they don't pass it by and take me to the north.

I awoke in a storm and there was Hamlet on his castle walls,
Balancing there to see how fast a body falls.
He'd been driven mad by poor Ophelia at last,
She'd forgotten to remember her forgotten past.
Then when we crossed the Sound in the frozen weather,
I saw them walk off in the snow to die together.

Why did you ever let her go away?
Asked the bells of La Chapelle as they passed away.
I couldn't bear to look at the Black Beast of Cologne,
Because it seemed to ask me why I let her go away alone.
They could have buried my soul in a box in Düsseldorf,
If they hadn't brought me here to the north.

THE END

If you would like to listen to the song Night Train,
whose lyrics you have just read in the book,
please type the following into your browser
http://www.gregorymotton.com/NightTrain.html